D1556076

THE
HISTORIC TÂF VALLEYS
Volume Three

From the Tâf confluence
at Cefn-Coed-y-Cymmer to Aberfan

Wellingtonia, with Cyfarthfa Castle Museum in the background (see pages 175-8) *Jack Evans*

THE
HISTORIC TÂF VALLEYS

Volume Three

From the Tâf confluence
at Cefn-Coed-y-Cymmer to Aberfan

GEOLOGY
SOCIAL AND INDUSTRIAL HISTORY
ALIEN PLANTS IN OUR MIDST

1986
Merthyr Tydfil and District Naturalists' Society
in conjunction with
D. Brown & Sons Limited, Cowbridge

© 1986 Merthyr Tydfil and District Naturalists' Society
ISBN 0 905928 59 8

DESIGNED AND PRINTED IN WALES BY
D. Brown & Sons Ltd., Bridgend, Mid Glamorgan

Contents

In the same series

THE HISTORIC TAFF VALLEY: QUAKERS YARD TO ABERFAN
by Mary Gillham, John Perkins and Clive Thomas
published September, 1979

THE HISTORIC TÂF VALLEYS Volume Two:
In the Brecon Beacon National Park
by John Perkins, Jack Evans and Mary Gillham
published December, 1982
Obtainable from: Administrative Office, Department of Extra Mural
Studies, 38 Park Place, Cardiff CF1 3BB *or* Jack Evans, Brynheulog,
Cilsanws, Cefn-Coed-y-Cymmer, Merthyr Tydfil at £5.95 *Post free.*

Foreword

From the President of the Society,
DOUGLAS W. THOMAS, F.R.C.S.

This third and final volume of *The Historic Tâf Valleys* is devoted to that section of the valley which extends from Cefn Coed-y-Cymmer to Aberfan and includes the town of Merthyr Tydfil.

John Perkins contributes another masterly series of geological walks for this area and shows how much Merthyr Tydfil's greatness was dependent on the local geology. He also explains the geological problems encountered during the building of the recently completed A470 expressway and how these were overcome.

Jack Evans has chosen to write on some of the local plants and trees and discusses their origins, the reputed therapeutic properties and cures effected by 'marvellous' herbs, and their not infrequent association with Welsh folk lore.

The major contribution to this book—the social and industrial history of Merthyr Tydfil—has been written by Clive Thomas. In a number of well-documented walks he explores the old residential areas, the iron-works sites and the mining localities, giving us in the process a vivid picture of what life in this famous town was like for the workers and their families during the Industrial Revolution.

Since that time many changes have taken place. The valley no longer echoes to the noise of heavy industry, the diesel engine has replaced steam and the air is clean and unpolluted. On the hillsides above the town one can sit and admire clear panoramic views of the valley. Few industrial relics are now visible, spoil tips are being levelled, trees are being planted and the original 'green and pleasant' land is re-emerging.

With the publication of Volume III 'The Historic Tâf Valleys' is complete. The three volumes provide a very comprehensive survey of the Tâf Valleys from their origins in the Brecon Beacons to Quakers Yard. The excellent series of planned walks—many in idyllic surroundings—should encourage us all to explore the countryside and enrich our knowledge and understanding of this most interesting and historic area.

Acknowledgements

The authors would like to thank all those who have helped in the production of the final volume of the trilogy of *The Historic Tâf Valleys*. The Merthyr Tydfil and District Naturalists' Society wishes to record its gratitude to the Merthyr Borough Council for its interest and financial support. An invaluable source of financial help has also been that from the Welsh Water Authority and the Michael Sobell Charitable Association.

Finally, the guidance and skill of Bob Whitaker and Anthony Green of D. Brown and Sons in piloting the books through the press has been of inestimable value.

Introduction

This is the third and final volume of the series covering the Tâf Valley from its twin sources in the Brecon Beacons down to the southern boundary of the Merthyr Tydfil Borough at Quakers' Yard.

Volume One had an obvious reason for its creation—the section between Quakers' Yard and Aberfan was then the least spoilt part of the valley left within the coalfield, a rural oasis. The new A470 dual carriageway has since been driven through it, but considerable stretches of its former character remain unharmed and much of the walk described in Volume One can still be followed.

In Volume Two we dealt with the Tâf Fawr and Tâf Fechan valleys from sources to confluence near Merthyr and, thus, with the Brecon Beacons National Park, areas not only unspoilt but guaranteed to remain so. The present volume seeks to complete this survey, filling in the central gap between the confluence of the two Tâfs at Cefn Coed y Cymmer, just north of Merthyr Tydfil, and Aberfan down valley. However, this is a task undertaken for more than the sake of mere completeness. Industrialised localities also have their own fascinating geological, natural and social history. Anyone who knows the coalfield country around Merthyr and down valley will agree that although the scars of its industrial past may seem overwhelming when viewed from the valley bottom, a walk up any local hillside swiftly takes one back to the original rural nature of the area.

The natural landscape can still be read by those who train themselves to look, and, from a hilltop vantage point, the industrial elements of the landscape are seen in their true proportion, as only one element in the true character of the valley.

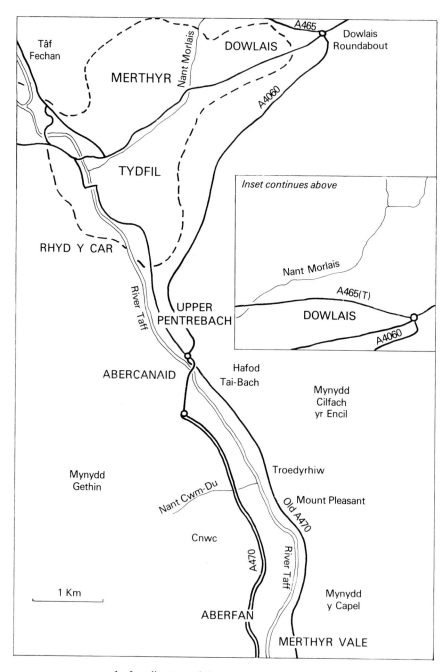

1 Locality map of the area covered in this book

Part One:
Geology

JOHN PERKINS

The Landscape

At the confluence at Cefn Coed the Tâf flows at 183 m (600 ft) above sea level. By the time it reaches Aberfan it has dropped to 130 m (425 ft). On the west the valley sides rise to 490 m (1,612 ft) on Mynydd Gethin, and on the east to 450 m (1,475 ft) on Mynydd Cilfach-yr-Encil above Troedyrhiw and 365 m (1,200 ft) at Mynydd y Capel, immediately east of Aberfan.

However, it is the plan of the valley which is its most interesting and revealing feature. The Tâf Fawr reaches its confluence with the Tâf Fechan through the relatively restricted section enclosed between Cefn Cil-Sanws and Craig Penmoelallt. (See *Historic Tâf Valleys*, Volume Two, pages 49-51 and 57.) There the river crosses the outcrops of the relatively resistant grits and conglomerates of the Millstone Grit. These are sloping south-east, off the Brecon Beacons.

By the time the river reaches the confluence, the more resistant beds have dipped below valley-floor level, to be replaced by less resistant sandstones

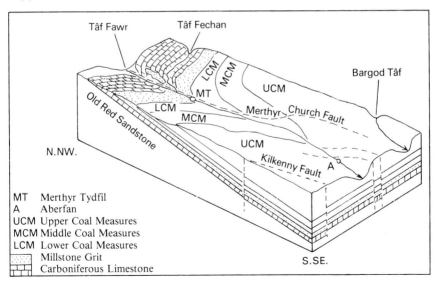

MT Merthyr Tydfil
A Aberfan
UCM Upper Coal Measures
MCM Middle Coal Measures
LCM Lower Coal Measures
Millstone Grit
Carboniferous Limestone

2 How the rock types control the shape of the lowland site of Merthyr Tydfil

11

and shales of the upper Millstone Grit beds and the Lower Coal Measures. The more easily eroded nature of the latter is evident from the valley form, which broadens dramatically into a great v-shape in plan, thus creating the triangular lowland which is now largely built over by Merthyr Tydfil and its suburbs.

South of the town the v-shaped lowland tapers across the Lower Coal Measures towards Troedyrhiw, its surrounding slopes scarred by innumerable ironstone and coal workings. These higher areas are formed in the Middle Coal Measures. The valley-sides gradually converge and from Troedyrhiw down to Aberfan the Tâf is once more enclosed, for the Middle Coal Measures contain many thick beds of more resistant sandstones. Thus, the area covered in this volume shows an intimate relationship between rock groups and valley form.

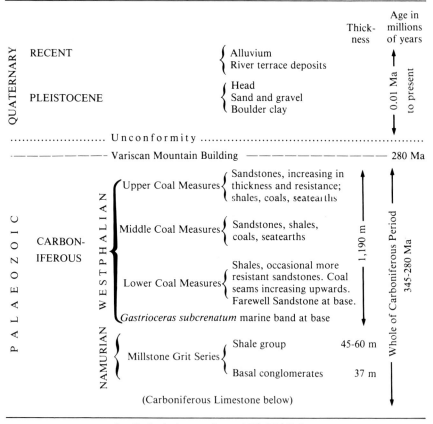

3 Geological succession, middle Tâf Valley

Crossing the Line

Before setting off to explore the various walks described below, it will be useful if the explorer has some idea of how this sequence of rocks came about. The preceding pages of the story have been described in Volume

Two, where the oldest rocks seen in the Brecon Beacons revealed a record of ancestral South Wales lying in latitudes south of the Equator. Semi-arid conditions obtained, (Volume Two, pages 19-20), and the rocks created then were the Devonian Old Red Sandstones, which now form the bulk of the area of the Brecon Beacons National Park.

From that period, 395-345 million years ago, South Wales (together with the rest of Britain and Europe) has drifted slowly across the Equator and up to its present-day latitude. In Volume Two we also saw how, as this drift took place, warm tropical seas gradually encroached northwards on to the semi-arid land. Running over the Old Red Sandstone deposits, it covered them with the next younger formation, the Carboniferous Limestone. (Volume Two, pages 19-22.)

However, recent research has shown that the new sea only extended as far as the northern areas of the present National Park, and beyond its shoreline Mid and North Wales remained land areas, experiencing semi-tropical weather conditions and, no doubt, being heavily eroded by streams and rivers, which were amply supplied by the high rainfall regime of such a climate.

The result was that deltas began to build up, spreading southwards from the coastline, flooding beds of quartz pebbles, gritty quartz grains, sands and muds into the shallow seas and thus burying the layers of the Carboniferous Limestone. It is with these beds, the layers of the Millstone Grit, that the present volume begins.

During the formation of the Millstone Grit, and of the Coal Measures which were to follow, there were two dominant geological processes at work in South Wales, (a) river delta formation, with growth of semi-tropical tree

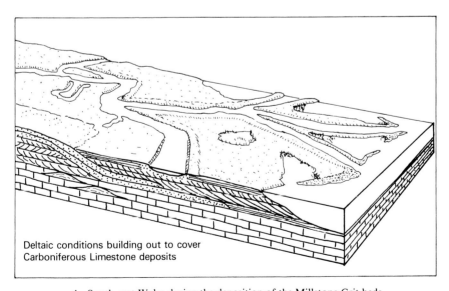

Deltaic conditions building out to cover
Carboniferous Limestone deposits

4   South-east Wales during the deposition of the Millstone Grit beds

13

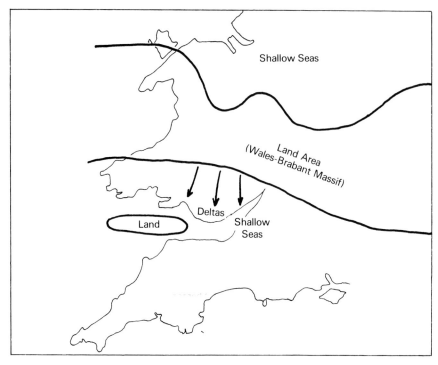

5 Distribution of land and sea in Wales during Millstone Grit and Lower Coal Measure deposition

fern forests, and (b) periodic interruptions to that activity by phases of accelerated subsidence. The repeated and accelerated subsidences often allowed the sea to temporarily return and drown the region again—until the deltas once again built out southwards and reclaimed the shallows.

The key to the geology of the area between Merthyr Tydfil and Aberfan lies in understanding these conditions. It is also the key to the area covered in Volume One, and, indeed, to the history of the South Wales coalfield in general.

Ups and Downs

While the mechanisms of continental drift, the process which carried South Wales northwards, through the tropics and up to its present position, are now well understood and have formed the basis of a revolution in the study of Geology over the last twenty years, the means by which blocks of the crust are elevated to become land areas, or, at other times, depressed beneath the sea during the drifting process are less well known. They continue to be the subject of much research and the answers may be sought in the earth's mantle, the zone beneath its crust.

However, whatever proves to be the cause, the effect is certainly well-documented in the local rock record. The key to the sequence of beds is the

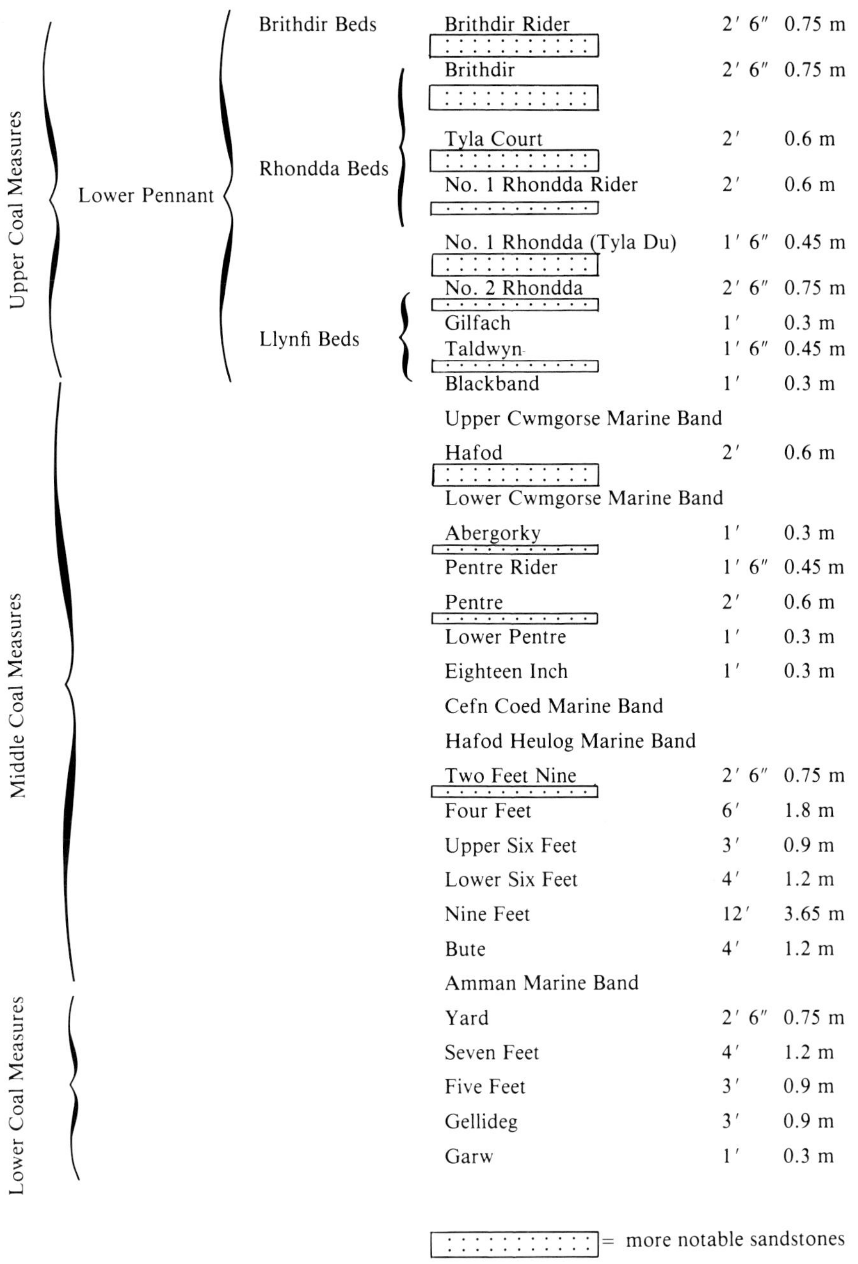

		Brithdir Beds	Brithdir Rider	2' 6"	0.75 m
			Brithdir	2' 6"	0.75 m
		Rhondda Beds	Tyla Court	2'	0.6 m
	Lower Pennant		No. 1 Rhondda Rider	2'	0.6 m
Upper Coal Measures			No. 1 Rhondda (Tyla Du)	1' 6"	0.45 m
		Llynfi Beds	No. 2 Rhondda	2' 6"	0.75 m
			Gilfach	1'	0.3 m
			Taldwyn	1' 6"	0.45 m
			Blackband	1'	0.3 m

Upper Cwmgorse Marine Band

Hafod	2'	0.6 m

Lower Cwmgorse Marine Band

Abergorky	1'	0.3 m
Pentre Rider	1' 6"	0.45 m
Pentre	2'	0.6 m
Lower Pentre	1'	0.3 m
Eighteen Inch	1'	0.3 m

Cefn Coed Marine Band

Hafod Heulog Marine Band

Two Feet Nine	2' 6"	0.75 m
Four Feet	6'	1.8 m
Upper Six Feet	3'	0.9 m
Lower Six Feet	4'	1.2 m
Nine Feet	12'	3.65 m
Bute	4'	1.2 m

Amman Marine Band

Yard	2' 6"	0.75 m
Seven Feet	4'	1.2 m
Five Feet	3'	0.9 m
Gellideg	3'	0.9 m
Garw	1'	0.3 m

(Middle Coal Measures and Lower Coal Measures labelled along left margin)

= more notable sandstones

6 Coal Seams of the District. Not drawn to scale; for that see 6 inch Geological Map, Sheet SO OO SE. Note increase in resistant sandstones towards top. In between all seams, in addition, siltstones, mudstones, seatearths, etc.

repetition of the two processes already mentioned, deltas building southwards, eventually filling the shallow seas and creating extensive coastal swamps which could be colonised by rich, tropical tree fern forests; then a renewed submergence, carrying the accumulated sediments under sea level for burial beneath a layer of marine mud. The next sequence of delta deposits built southwards again and eventually allowed new forest growth. In other words, the activity was cyclic, and so the repetitive 'layer-cake' of the Coal Measures was created.

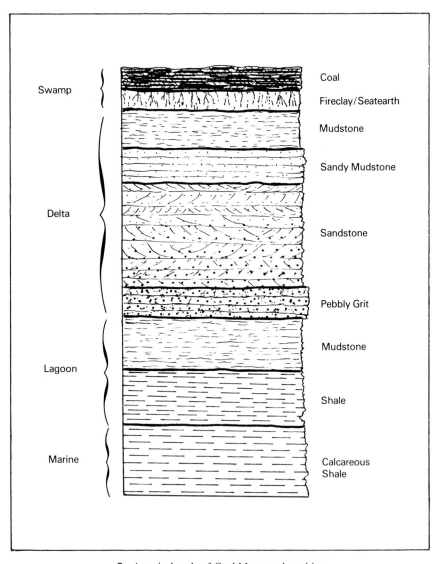

7   A typical cycle of Coal Measure deposition

Each new submergence by the sea was marked by a layer of marine mud and fossils (these layers are known as marine bands); each successful reclamation by the deltas culminated in a renewed forest growth. It was the next submergence again which began the process of converting a forest's peaty debris into a new seam of coal.

These repetitive, cyclic deposits are known to geologists as cyclothems, each representing a unit of Carboniferous time. A typical example is illustrated.

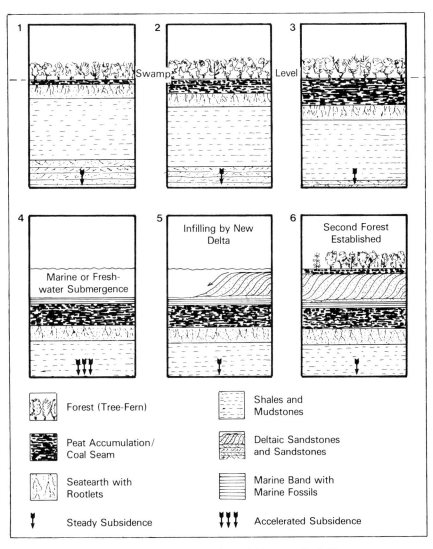

8 Formation of coal seams with variable rates of subsidence

17

Consider the nature of the subsidence for a moment, for this feature explains much about the origin of the cyclothems and about the varying thickness of the individual coal seams. Several metres of rotten swamp vegetation are necessary to form each 0.3 m (1 ft) coal seam. The implication is clear. Subsidence must have continued slowly all the time, proceeding at just the right rate during the accumulation to allow forest growth and further addition on the surface. In no other way could such thicknesses of rotted vegetation be achieved.

On occasions, however, the subsidence speeded up, stopping the addition of more peat debris at the surface and carrying what was already available below the water surface for eventual burial by other sediments and conversion into a coal seam. This accelerated subsidence was sometimes complete enough to allow a fresh inundation of the area by the sea and the formation of a new marine band. On other occasions it was only partial and no new marine band was formed before the next sequence of delta deposits arrived.

Down in the Forest

Coal formation requires an abundant supply of rotting vegetation and a subsequent history of burial and compression, plus a suitable structure where the seam can then survive, e.g., when folded down into a basin. Clearly, coal cannot be found in rocks older than the appearance of abundant plant life on earth, neither, on the other hand, can it be very good coal if the deposit is too young in age to have had the benefit of being involved in some structural activity.

South Wales has an important place in the study of fossil plants and in

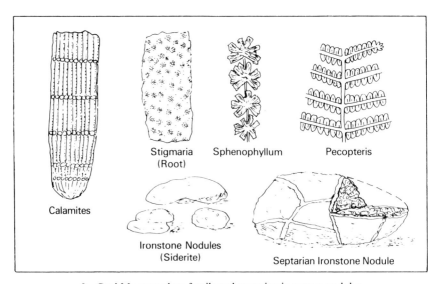

Stigmaria
(Root)

Sphenophyllum

Pecopteris

Calamites

Ironstone Nodules
(Siderite)

Septarian Ironstone Nodule

9   Coal Measure plant fossils and septarian ironstone nodules

this region their history has been researched back into Devonian and Silurian age beds.

There can be few miners' families who have not seen some fragment of fern leaf or tree trunk brought up from the pit, a record in carbon of those long-buried tropical tree ferns. Today, the most beautiful specimens come from the great opencast sites being worked along the North Crop of the coalfield, all of them outside the district covered in this book. Plant fossils can still turn up, however, on the older more weathered coal tips and it is useful to realise that though they are beautifully detailed, the fern leaves are not the actual fossilised leaf but carbonised impressions of it, i.e., they are properly known as plant compression fossils.

Studied in detail they reveal that the plants functioned in exactly the same ways as modern plants. Although there were insects about, however, plants of that period reproduced themselves by means of spores. There were no plants which flowered and depended on insects for their pollination until after Carboniferous times.

Pennant Sandstones and Ironstones

There are two other important aspects of the history of Carboniferous times. Towards the top of the Coal Measure accumulation, greater thicknesses of quartz sandstones were deposited, the resistant layers known as the Pennant Sandstones. These can be seen on the top of the eastern valleyside. Together with other sandstones in the sequence they provide the principal building stones of the district, the material from which the long rows of terraced houses were constructed. The Pennant Sandstones account for most of the ridge tops throughout the coalfield, and they cap the valley sides here as the Tâf continues southwards towards Troedyrhiw.

The other feature is the importance of the ironstone deposits in the Coal Measures. The iron occurs as iron carbonate nodules of the mineral called siderite. These are about 30% iron ore and they formed the original basis of the South Wales iron industry. They were worked on the hillsides of the North Crop when ironworks first sprang up along the Heads of the Valleys area.

Millions and millions of tonnes of these nodules still lie within the coalfield's rocks, but they are less rich than ore from overseas sources, for which the steelworks were drawn to their present coastal sites with direct import facilities. Today no one would contemplate the costly business of extracting the remaining local ironstone nodules—it would mean literally quarrying away most of the coalfield, for the nodules occur in the beds between the coal seams, in the shaly muds. How did they get there?

Remember that the deltas and swamps lay to the south of areas of Mid and North Wales which had remained land since Devonian times and where the surface rock would still have been the iron-rich Old Red Sandstones or older materials. Iron was eroded from these sources and carried down in the rivers building the Millstone Grit and Coal Measure deltas over South Wales. If the iron was carried away in a reduced state as ferrous carbonate or bi-carbonate, on entering the swamps and deltas it could have been precipitated as a result of the abstraction of carbon dioxide (CO^2) by plants. A second possibility is that the iron, which would be positively charged, was transported as ferric oxide. On coming into contact with negatively charged muds it would also have been precipitated; and could have been reduced to the ferrous state once it was enclosed within the sediment.

The nodules certainly seem to be concentrated in bands or thin continuous beds, and the greatest concentrations occur in places where shale beds rest on coal seams, deposits often representing stagnant lagoons or freshwater ponds on the tops of the deltas.

Anyone examining these red-brown nodules today will soon discover that they also owe something of their shape to the processes which eventually compacted and hardened all the sediments into rock. Many have later been split and fissured. They are known as septarian nodules. Their fissures appear now as veins or walls (septa), filled with other minerals.

Calcite or dolomite are the commonest minerals in these whitish/orangey veins, and if you split a nodule open there may be cavities with small but perfect crystals of pyrite (iron sulphide), blende (zinc sulphide), chalcopyrite (copper sulphide) or galena (lead sulphide), sitting on the other mineral of the walls. Less commonly the principal vein mineral may be ankerite, a light orangey-brown carbonate of iron. If you are very lucky you may open a nodule with a bunch of fine gold 'hairs' in it, the mineral millerite, a nickel ore, popularly known as hair pyrites.

Collisions and Mountains

The formation of the Coal Measures and their attendant coal seams and ironstones ended with the close of the Carboniferous period, 280 million

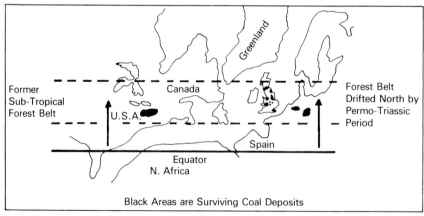

10 The British, European and North American coalfields are remnants of an equatorial forest belt, here seen drifted North (dashed lines) at the time of Pangaea

years ago. A great collision of the continents occurred then, buckling and folding all the South Wales sediments that had accumulated in the Devonian and Carboniferous periods, affecting the Old Red Sandstones, the Carboniferous Limestone, Millstone Grit, and Coal Measures, locally creating a great basin, the structure of the South Wales coalfield.

This was an important event, the necessary burial, folding and increases in temperature and pressure required to convert the forest remains within the rocks to coal.

The type of coal produced results from the type of plant material involved, i.e., was it bark, leaves, etc? It is also affected by the degree of burial and compaction. This determines the coal's 'rank', i.e., where it stands in the series of coals which begin with peat and, marked by increasing carbon content and reductions in volatile content, progress through the brown coals or lignites to sub-bituminous, bituminous and, finally, anthracite. In the first, evidence of plant material is abundant, but at the other end of the series, in anthracite, nearly all trace of plant debris has gone.

No rock record is preserved in the middle Tâf valley after the mountain building event, but clearly many things must have occurred to eventually shape the present landscape. At some stage the river system of the Tâf came into being. It appears to be a superimposed river, i.e., one which was eroded down into the coalfield structure from above. The traditional theory is described in Volume One, page 37, and depends on the presence of some younger rock layer, over which the Tâf and the other rivers of South East Wales began their south-southeasterly courses, eventually wearing that younger cover away and lowering their courses into the older rocks beneath. The one subsequent event for which some evidence remains is the effect of glaciation on the area during the recent Ice Age.

So the physical landscape of the Tâf between its confluence and Aberfan is the result of:

(i) The changing conditions during the deposition of the rocks in Carboniferous times.

(ii) The continental collision and mountain building which formed the coalfield structure at the close of Carboniferous times.

(iii) The long interval since, during which the present landscape was eroded into and differentially weathered those rock layers.

(iv) The modifications caused to that landscape by the recent and disruptive event of the Ice Age.

The Ice Age

During the Ice Age most of Britain was covered by ice caps and glaciers, with the mountains of Wales acting as one of the local gathering grounds and feeding valley glaciers around the margins of the ice cap. Among the former were the glaciers moving down into the valleys of the coalfield, where through routes from the Brecon Beacons had already been created by

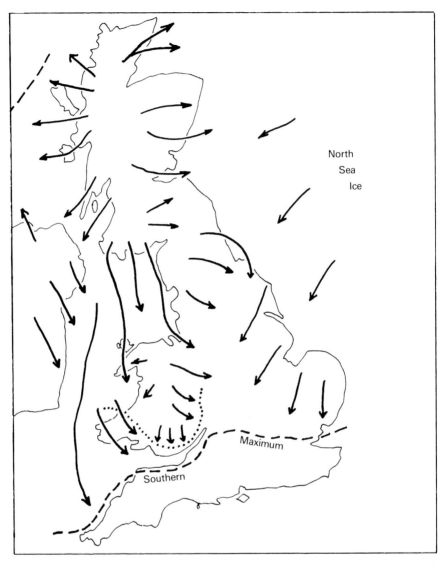

11 Maximum extent of the Ice-Sheets in Glacial Periods of the Anglian (dashed lines) and Devensian (shown by dots for South Wales only). Arrows show direction of ice movement

previous river erosion, as in the case of the Tâf. Elsewhere in the coalfield, closed valley heads, e.g., the Rhondda, generated their own local glacier sources.

The Ice Age was a complex and multiple event. It contained four cold phases, marked by southward advances of the glaciers, each time to a different southern maximum, and astonishingly warm climatic phases in between (interglacials) when the climate became like that of parts of East

Africa today. With land access available right across Europe, the migration of quite unexpected animals into the area was made possible. Evidence for the dramatic faunal changes which followed the climatic fluctuations comes from two main sources: (a) the remains of animals from either the cold or the warm phases which were trapped when they fell into underground caves and cavities, and (b) the remains of animals trapped or hunted by early man and found around his old habitation sites. Again, many of these were caves.

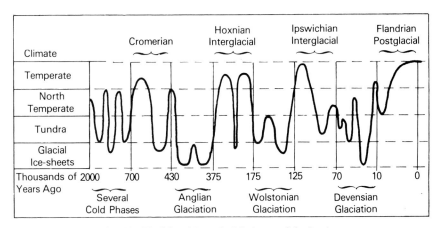

12   The Glacial and Interglacial phases of the Ice Age

In the cold advances man hunted reindeer, small mammals like rabbit or hare, woolly mammoth and woolly rhinoceros. In the warmed periods he could chase the straight-tusked elephant, fallow deer and giant ox and see cave lions and hyaena about.

The immediate area of this study contains no limestone beds or caves of the kind described, but it is important to know that these were the probable local patterns of activity. There are, however, plenty of archaeological remains from periods since the Ice Age, hut circles, etc., when the present climatic recovery once again made the area more habitable by man (see Volume Two). Thus evidence from a wider area has to be used to interpret some aspects of the Tâf valley during the Ice Age. A useful source of local evidence comes from the changes in vegetation which have accompanied the post-glacial warming, and these are described later in this book.

What geological evidence is there for the Ice Age in the middle Tâf valley? The area came within the ice-covered zone at each of the glacial advances, so the evidence of any one advance would have been destroyed by the next and what remains in the area now are the loose drift deposits from the last cold phase, plus all the modifications made to them since, as river erosion has returned to the valley.

Most of the drift is what geologists call boulder clay or moraine, i.e., ill-assorted masses of finely ground rock material, very poorly bedded or

23

layered and containing masses of randomly-sized boulders. This is ground moraine, the debris which was being ground along within the bottom ice of the glaciers, helping to act as abrasive grits and achieve further valley erosion. This type of material is predominant in the upper and middle Tâf. Further down the valley there are additional features, more sandy beds, material sorted out from the moraines and carried down by the river; and beyond the Tâf gorge at Tongwynlais the great lowland spread of fluvio-glacial gravels on which much of Cardiff is built. This is the flood-plain area where the Tâf has deposited all the glacially eroded material which it has managed to flush out of its higher reaches since the end of the glacial activity.

Up in the area of the present study the two most dangerous legacies of the Ice Age are undoubtedly the oversteepening of valley-sides, leading to landslip occurrence, and the situations where drift deposits cover natural spring lines, building up water pressures within otherwise well-jointed and permeable sandstone beds, and converting them into what are called confined aquifers.

The Shaping of the Hillsides

Three main factors contribute to the hill-slopes formed in the middle Tâf valley:

(i)   The parent rock type, i.e., the variable Coal Measure succession of shales, sandstones, coal seams, seatearths.

(ii) The response to, and movement of ground water through this sequence.

(iii) The various methods of erosion which have sculpted the surface of the valley, principally the river and glacial erosion.

Included in the third group we must place all the ongoing processes of land-slipping, soil flow, soil creep, etc., which are continuing to erode and modify the valley-sides. Many of the latter processes are the legacy of the recent Ice Age and it is undoubtedly true to describe the valley as still in the process of 'recovery' from that event. But then, what is normality in Geology? Any process, albeit one which occurs more rarely, is surely part of overall geological activity.

Parent rock type

The resistance to erosion of the differing beds in a Coal Measure sequence is important. The quartz-grained Pennant sandstones are the most resistant. Their major joint systems represent their weak point, allowing erosion to widen these clefts, or, in the case of ice, to heave them open. The sandstones persist as resistant blocks and if, eventually, these are whittled down and removed, they form the bulk of the river bed boulder and gravel debris.

The shales, with their randomly layered character, are more easily removed and, once carried away by the river, are soon broken into tiny

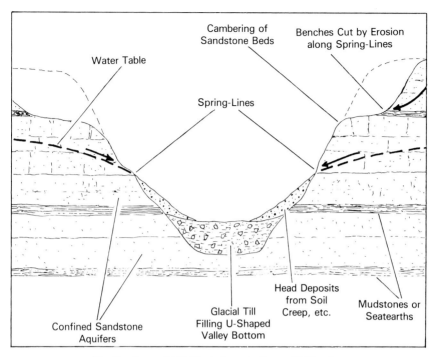

13   Benches and hillside drainage in the coalfield valleys

fragments. Least resistant of all to erosion are the coal seams, which soon degrade and often become barely traceable along the hillsides since their erosion allows the beds above them to settle or camber, coming down on those below to obscure the coal outcrop.

The seatearths, especially the fireclays, below the coal seams play their most important role in controlling the movement of groundwater within the hillsides. This is because of their less permeable nature. Groundwater can easily descend through the well-jointed sandstones, but when a less permeable layer, e.g., a fireclay or a shale, is encountered below, the water is forced to migrate laterally, emerging along the hillside as a series of springs. These erode the slope along that line, and help to set off the cambering described above. Benches develop, and on the top of the sandstone involved in the cambering, gulls or fissures open out (see walk on summit of Cnwc, described later).

It takes practice to recognise all the benches which may be present on a local hillside. The more major ones, with thick beds of Pennant sandstones between them are obvious, but many less well-developed ones can be hard to spot. This is because they are, of course, covered by debris from all these processes of change. The eroded material which is slowly but relentlessly being moved downhill to the river piles up on the bench surfaces and thus tends to mask their presence. The consequences for tip safety are described below.

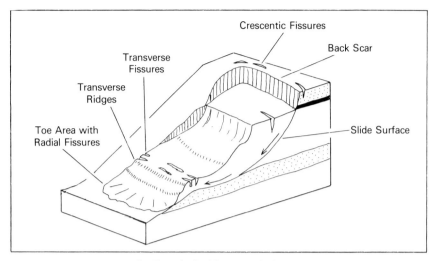

14 The principal features of a landslip

Landslips, Natural and Man-made

Hardly a winter passes without an alarm somewhere in the coalfield about hillside safety, and sometimes the evacuation of threatened houses below the affected area. Why is the coalfield so prone to these geological hazards? Part of the answer lies in the variable rock sequences and the movement of groundwater already referred to above. A share of the blame must also rest with the Ice Age, however. Unlike river erosion, where the river's main task is to cut the valley bottom while its tributaries, springs and the processes described above attend to the slopes around it, ice fills much of the valley and can grind away at the higher slopes equally as well as it can deepen and scour the valley floor. Ice removes rock spurs and straightens and deepens the valley to such an extent that, when the ice has gone, the valley-side may literally be too steep to remain stable. Mass movements and landslips follow, as the valley adjusts back to the more gentle angles of slope characteristic of river regimes.

1. Nant Morlais

This walk on the high moorlands NE of Dowlais Top provides an opportunity to see the sequence of rocks which form the Millstone Grit, i.e., the deltaic beds which succeeded and covered the Carboniferous Limestones (Volume Two, pages 64-79), and began the swampy conditions which were to lead to the formation of the Coal Measures.

At Dowlais Top roundabout on the Heads of the Valleys road, the explorer stands on Lower Coal Measures with large opencast sites visible in the Middle Coal Measures to the south. To the north, on the Lower Coal Measures themselves, the Asda Superstore stands on the site of old surface

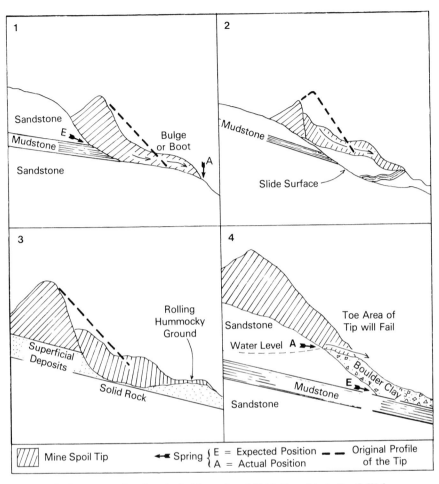

15   Four examples of geological hazards to hillside tip safety in South Wales.
1. Tip placed on natural bench covers springs.
2. Tip placed on bench caused by natural landslip re-activates it.
3. Load of a tip placed on weak superficial deposits displaces them.
4. Impermeable boulder clay displaces spring from expected position and endangers toe of tip.

workings for ironstone. Glacial drifts cover the moorland around here, giving it a wet, reed-grown aspect.

Follow the old railway track west and north towards Pantyscallog. The track leads over the Lower Coal Measures towards the Nant Morlais brook where the rocks can be traced down into the Millstone Grit. Because you are walking down the succession the first rock encountered is the Farewell Sandstone, forming a broad SW facing spur to the hillside and marked by the site of the old cottages and houses at Pen-y-garn-ddu.

The Farewell Sandstone is so named because it marks the boundary between the Coal Measures and the Millstone Grit below. It was the lowest bed in the mines; beneath it you could not hope to find coal or ironstone,

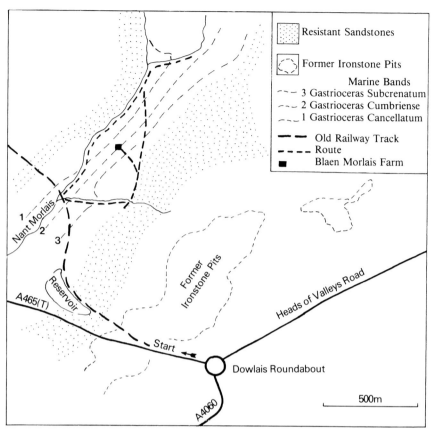

16 Route for the Nant Morlais walk

hence its name. Opinion is divided about its origin, some saying that it was so named as the farewell to coal, others as the farewell to ironstone.

Between Pen-y-garn-ddu and the bridge where the old railway crossed the Nant Morlais, one walks, without visible exposures, over a series of Millstone Grit shales, sandstones and marine bands. At the bridge the stream intersects the outcrop of the *Gastrioceras cancellatum* marine band. Turn upstream and in 400m enter a small gorge, its walls revealing the blackish shales and thin quartz sandstones of the Millstone Grit sequence. The stream flows along the boundary between these less resistant beds and the underlying tougher and thickly-bedded basal sandstones of the Millstone Grit, which here form the northwest bank. No doubt the brook has evolved along this boundary, slipping southwards off the dip-slope formed by the top of the sandstones and, in so doing, cutting into the SE bank, stripping off and revealing the softer black shales.

Walk up the gorge, examining the shale and thin sandstone exposures, to the stream junction about 60m further up. Follow the branch coming in from the east. This is a good section to search for fossil evidence and about

150m from the junction the outcrop of both the *Gastrioceras cancellatum* marine band and a bed containing the bivalve shell *Carbonicola* can be found.

Return to the junction and about 100m below it take the track leading back south towards Blaen Morlais Farm. 200m from the junction with the track from the farm itself, a small brook flows west down to the Nant Morlais, joining it at the track/old railway bridge described earlier. The small tributary cuts down the succession, running over the very fossiliferous outcrop of the *Gastrioceras subcrenatum* marine band 130m west of the track and then, 140m further west again, equally well exposing the *Gastrioceras cancellatum* marine band. Here then, in the Nant Morlais and its tributaries, there are fine illustrations of the Millstone Grit delta deposits which built southwards, and of their occasional submergence and the formation of marine bands, setting the scene and the style for the sedimentation and subsidences which were to lead to the formation of the South Wales coalfield. There is one other walk to be made before the explorer leaves these Millstone Grit sequences and enters the coalfield proper.

2. Pwll Wat, Merthyr Church Fault and the confluence

Start near the A470 bridge over the Tâf Fechan at Cefn Coed y Cymmer. Using the smaller bridge just upstream, cross to the east bank and then walk down river. (The walk on page 75, Volume Two, starts here but goes upstream.) A splendid tall limekiln is soon encountered on the left bank, its twin archways fed by three wells and its top rising to a charging platform level with the main road above. The kiln is built of the same Carboniferous Limestone which was burned in it, but the hillside against which it stands is in sandstones of the Millstone Grit beds.

Lime-burning was practiced for both agricultural and industrial purposes, e.g., centuries ago any major building work involved constructing a kiln near-by to produce sufficient lime for the mortar required. For agriculture, manuring the land by the application of lime was a practice which reached its greatest popularity in the period 1750-1850. However, this kiln was no doubt constructed for the iron industry, producing lime for flux and other purposes.

The only reason for burning limestone was, of course, to reduce it to a powder, i.e., limekilns preceded the ability to build the sort of crushing plants on which modern quarries depend.

The kiln charging platform at the top was on a level with the present main road, and there the mouths of the three wells were filled with alternating layers of fuel and limestone lumps. The platform is now very overgrown and no details of the platform top can be seen. The wells have long since been filled in with rubbish.

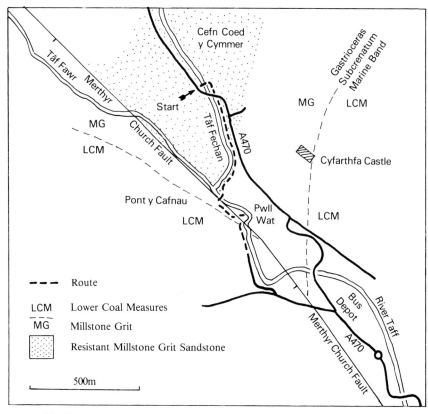

17 Sketch map of the Merthyr Church Fault and route for walk to Pwll Wat

However, down here on the river bank, the firegrates at the bases of the wells, through which the burned lime was withdrawn, can be seen at the backs of the kiln arches. There are two archways so the central well could discharge into either. Walk in to the inner end of one archway and notice the smaller side passages along the back of the kiln. These ensured that the wells were standing free of the hillside behind, i.e., that no ground-water could seep into the wells, with the consequent risks of steam generation and explosion.

Continue down the river bank and notice the old leat which ran into the Cyfarthfa Ironworks. This pathway was once the main route into Merthyr! Here the Tâf Fechan flows exactly in the direction of the dip of the rocks and at two localities slabs of Millstone Grit sandstones can be seen in the river bed, dipping 8° SSE. Cross a stile and turn west, following the river to its confluence with the Tâf Fawr and Pont y Cafnau. The latter, an old works bridge, provides a fine view of the confluence, just upstream, with the western bank of the Tâf Fawr bounded by an old white slag tip from the Cyfarthfa Ironworks. Also visible upstream is the Cwm Ffrwd viaduct (Volume Two, page 52), on the Heads of the Valleys road, while just

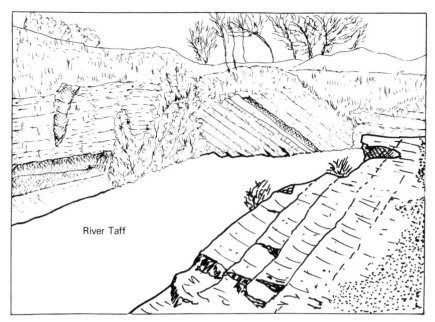

River Taff

18 The Merthyr Church Fault at Pwll Wat with Cumbriense shales, left bank, and Cumbriense quartzite, right bank. All these beds are part of the Millstone Grit. Distant bank: beds thrown down by the fault movement

downstream of the bridge, on the east bank, is the former water turbine house of the Merthyr Electric Tramway Company.

Cross Pont y Cafnau and walk down the west bank of the united streams towards Pwll Wat, for, geologically speaking, this is an exciting locality. Here, one of the myriads of NW-SE faults which cut the structure of the coalfield, the Merthyr Church Fault, is exposed. No doubt it controlled the original cutting of the Tâf Fawr valley. As the river leaves the Brecon Beacons and passes through Merthyr it follows the fault closely. The figure shows the details of the fault here at Pwll Wat; it can also be seen, on a broader canvas, on the walk east of Troedyrhiw (see below).

The source streams of the Tâf generally seem to be spelt that way, i.e., Tâf, but it also seems to be convention to talk of the Taff for the united stream, so, having now reached the main river, the remaining walks will be in the Taff valley!

3. Rhyd y Car

This walk is one of the most useful for an over-view of the local geological situation. Start from the car park of the Rhyd y Car leisure centre, near the site of the old Rhyd y Car mine whose shafts were located on the outcrops of the Seven Feet and Nine Feet coals and were sunk to the Gellideg and Garw seams below. The pit was therefore working in the Lower Coal Measures.

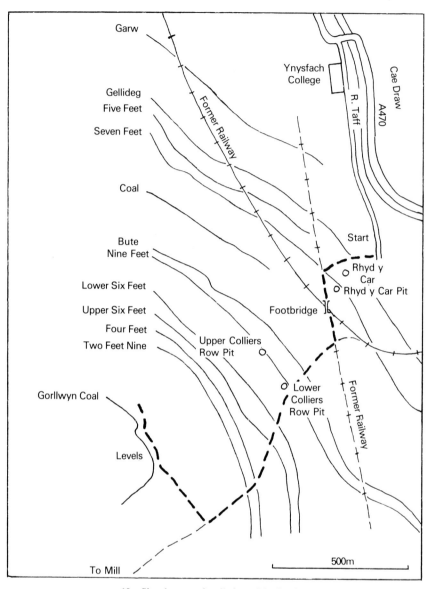

19 Sketch map of walk from Rhyd y Car

The walk works west and south, passing up the tremendously damaged hillsides on to the Middle Coal Measures and the closely spaced seams of the Bute, Nine Feet, Upper and Lower Six Feet and Two Feet Nine coals. There are no exposures but the scale of the former activity is self-evident and closely followed directions are needed to stay on the route and reach the northern slopes of the Nant Canaid valley beyond.

From the leisure centre car park walk west, keeping to the left of the stream and leaving a bungalow to your right. Proceed up to an old Pennant sandstone square-built mine structure. Pass close to the right of this and in a few metres bear left (south) along a former railway track to a more recent footbridge over another old railway (046052). About 120m beyond that a lane crosses the path. Turn right and follow it uphill towards the south-west.

There are now two alternatives. By keeping to the track the explorer eventually reaches a gate, to the left of which are the remains of an old watermill. Beyond the gate, the track continues west up to the former Hendre-fawr farm, where an old date stone, inscribed 1796, can be found among the ruins of the house and barns.

However, the more interesting walk begins before reaching the gate and the ruined mill. It is difficult to spot, but, about 300m before the gate there is an indistinct path leading off to the right. It starts near the crest of the track, before the track starts to drop towards the ruined mill. Running uphill towards the northwest, the path rises to the 275m (900ft) contour and the outcrop of the Gorllwyn coal. Walking along the contour towards the north and west, one follows a magnificent series of drift workings, with the old spoil tips to the right and the entrances to the drifts in alcoves cut back into the wooded hillside to the left. The first group of spoil tips, trammed out to the right, provide a superb overlook for the whole of the Merthyr area, including most of the areas described in this book and the more southerly ones dealt with in Volume Two, which form the scenic backdrop to the north.

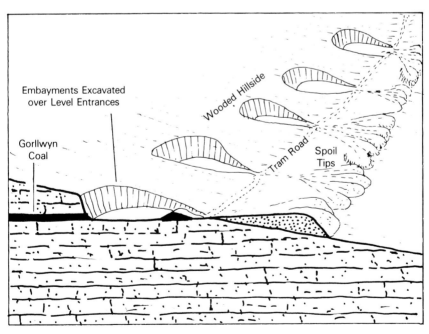

20   Diagrammatic view of mine levels on the Gorllwyn Coal

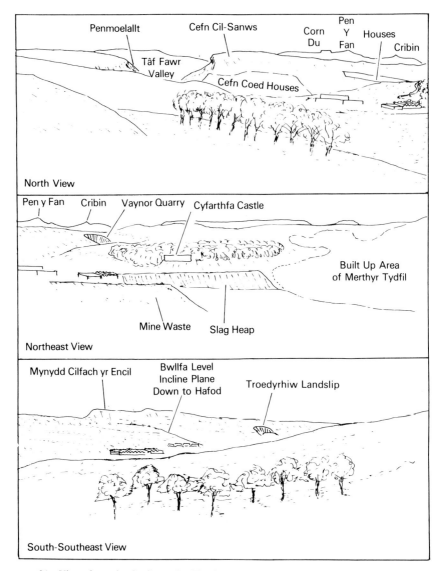

North View

Penmoelallt — Cefn Cil-Sanws — Corn Du — Pen Y Fan — Houses — Cribin — Tâf Fawr Valley — Cefn Coed Houses

Northeast View

Pen y Fan — Cribin — Vaynor Quarry — Cyfarthfa Castle — Built Up Area of Merthyr Tydfil — Mine Waste — Slag Heap

South-Southeast View

Mynydd Cilfach yr Encil — Bwllfa Level Incline Plane Down to Hafod — Troedyrhiw Landslip

21   Views from the Gorllwyn Coal levels to North, North-East and South-Southeast

Looking north, examine the distant view of the Tâf Fawr coming down through the Millstone Grit conglomerate outcrops of Cefn Cil-Sanws and Penmoelallt, and notice how these hillsides differ in level, being displaced by the fault along the valley there. As the Millstone Grit descends towards the viewpoint and passes below Merthyr Tydfil itself, so the role of the less resistant Millstone Grit shales and the Lower Coal Measures becomes apparent in the development of the great triangular lowlands around the town. Turning then towards the east, the southward tapering of the lowland towards the Hoover factory and Troedyrhiw is apparent, as the Taff again

34

becomes more enclosed. The hillsides opposite, scarred by innumerable coal and ironstone workings, rise through the Lower and Middle Coal Measures and are finally capped, and partly preserved of course, by the strong Pennant sandstone ridge-tops which narrow the valley as it flows on further south into the coalfield. This is a really superb viewpoint, demonstrating not only the geology but also much of the history of the district, graphically revealing how the early ironworks had everything on hand, coal, ironstone, limestone for flux, and the river valley to provide a route for the canal, and, eventually, the railways, to get the products away to the coast. The boom economy which followed, with all its attendant human horrors (see later sections), could never hope to last indefinitely however, for the whole economic edifice was based on a quicksand, its dependence on extractive industry and, therefore, ultimately on finite resources.

4. Eastern Valley-Side above Troedyrhiw

This is a longer walk up the east side of the Taff valley, starting from the regraded tip land north of Troedyrhiw. Coming by car, park in the industrial estate west of the old A470, near the B & Q superstore. Like all its neighbours, as far north as the embankment and bridge of the new A470, the superstore stands on regraded colliery waste, moved here from the east side of the main road, i.e., from the old tips of the South Dyffryn Colliery.

Cross the road to the stile by the gate opposite B & Q, where a public footpath leads on to the hillside. The track curves upwards to the right, its hardcore revealing all the local rock materials, fragments of black shale, reddish-brown ironstones and coal, as well as local slag. Notice the manholes for the internal drainage system installed inside the tip material still left on this side of the road, to ensure that it remains stable.

Once on top of the rise, head straight for the base of the natural hill-slope to the east and cross the drainage ditch at the rear of the tip. This was installed to prevent any surface water running off the hill from entering the waste material.

An old incline track rises southwards up the slope, and a further scramble upwards from it leads to the lower of a line of old quarries. As you ascend to them, you pass over the outcrops of the Taldwyn and No. 2 Rhondda coals and you may spot the tell-tale depressions caused by the old drift of crop workings which mark their outcrops. Above them there is a resistant sandstone bed, a pennant-type sandstone, and hence the line of quarries which were worked to provide building stone. Mine shafts existed on the floor of the southern quarry at one time and the present floor has clearly been filled in and levelled with mine waste. The faces of this more southerly quarry, known as Troedyrhiw Quarry, provide deeper and more useful sections, demonstrating the bedding and jointing of these river-laid quartz sandstones. Large sets of cross-beds can be seen, demonstrating the point bars of the once ever-changing river bends, particularly in the block left

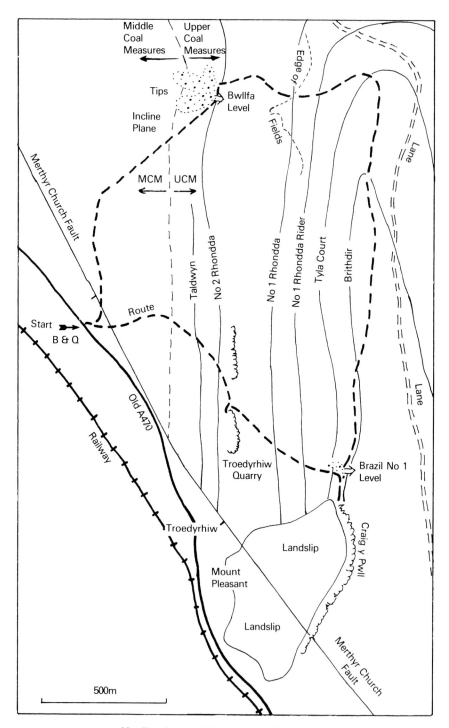

22 Sketch map of the walk east of Troedyrhiw

between the two entrances to the quarry. The overall dip of the beds is 6-8° to the southeast, i.e., slightly into the face of the hillside.

At the north end of Troedyrhiw Quarry the overlying shales are just exposed. Leaving at that end of the quarry, skirt the edge of the workings, keeping well away from the edge, and continue southeastwards uphill. As you rise up the slope three or four lines of dimples, old crop workings, mark the positions of the No. 1 Rhondda, No. 1 Rhondda Rider, Tyla Court and Brithdir coals. All have their attendant small spoil dumps and in several cases their adits are still open. Never enter them.

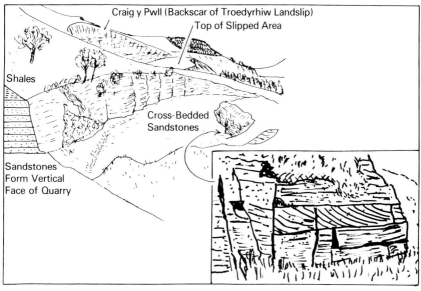

23   Troedyrhiw Quarry

A huge natural cliff of sandstones, in two prominent beds with a shale parting in between, can be seen ahead. It is known as Craig y Pwll and is the back scar of a huge landslip. Make for the level of the Brithdir seam, located by the little cone-shaped tip of the old Brazil level at the top of the slope. Then you can walk south along the Brithdir outcrop to a vantage point on the northern boundary of the landslip. The rolling hummocky ground extending down to the village of Troedyrhiw below is unmistakable, and the area of slumped land can be clearly determined. It is obviously a rotational slip and it probably occurred in the wetter climatic and ground-water conditions immediately after the Ice Age, when glaciers had left the Taff valley with oversteepened hillsides. But there is an additional villain in the piece here. The Merthyr Church Fault, previously described in walk 2, is also involved. It runs on down the Taff valley from Merthyr through upper and lower Pentre-bach and Tai Bach, and, where the main road enters the village, into Troedyrhiw. It then begins to diverge from the valley bottom

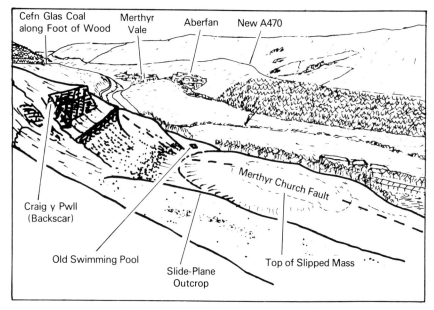

Cefn Glas Coal along Foot of Wood

Merthyr Vale

Aberfan

New A470

Craig y Pwll (Backscar)

Old Swimming Pool

Slide-Plane Outcrop

Merthyr Church Fault

Top of Slipped Mass

24 Troedyrhiw Postglacial rotational landslip

and continues southeast across the slopes above Chapel Street, and then across the hillside above Mount Pleasant, i.e., there it crosses the lower end of the landslip. No doubt its presence was a contributory weakness.

Notice how none of the crop workings have followed the coals into the disrupted and chaotic geology within the landslip. Other features to spot are the backscar and the gully at its foot which marks the outcrop of the slide plane of the slip. When such rotational slips occur, the upper surface of the fallen block is often left with a backtilt, allowing water to accumulate there, directly above the outcrop of the slide plane. Thus the water continues to lubricate the slip and keep it on the move. Spotting the water available here, local miners built a swimming pool for the village during the depression of the early 1930's and it can still be seen below the southern end of the back scar. It is now disused.

From the backscar of Craig y Pwll to the toe of the slip it is nearly 500 m, and the higher houses and streets of Troedyrhiw are actually built on the toe area. Measured north-south along the hillside the slip reaches 700 m. Return along the Brithdir seam outcrop, passing a number of old crop workings, and reach the little pyramidal waste tip of the old Brazil No. 1 level. Beyond it other crop workings are visible, extending a long way northwards along the slopes of Mynydd Cilfach-yr-Encil. Looking that way you are, of course, looking up dip, so the lines of crop workings rise, getting gradually nearer and nearer to the ridge top, and eventually curving eastwards around the far end of the ridge. The outcrops then return south along its far side in Cwm Bargoed.

Reducing the gradient of the climb by walking northeastwards from the Brazil level, make for the ridge top. The summit is formed of Brithdir Sandstones and these are part of the Upper Coal Measures. These beds are quartz sandstones, Pennant material, but very thin-bedded and their tumbled blocks look like piles of pancakes. Examine the various blocks and notice how the thin layers are in different attitudes, i.e., the rocks are cross-bedded, formed in the beds of meandering, changing rivers.

Due to the well-developed jointing, erosion has been able to heave many blocks out of their original position. Frost or ice action would be able to achieve this, especially in the period just after the Ice Age. Water, expanding into ice, has sufficient power to heave quite large rock masses out of alignment.

Walk over to the east side of the ridge to view Cwm Bargoed. Again old crop workings are numerous and help to pick out the outcrops of the various seams. The most prominent on the far side of the valley are those on the Tyla Court and Brithdir seams. These include some working private drift mines, on the hillside just above the mineral railway line.

25 Cross-bedded and frost-heaved blocks of Pennant sandstones, summit of Mynydd Cilfach-yr-Encil

Return to the ridge top and walk to its northern end. Crossing bilberry moor, the number of eroded blocks gradually decreases, and at the northern end most of those that existed have clearly been carried away by the ice sheets as they pushed south, passing along both sides of the ridge. At the cairn circle, 079039, turn west-southwest and make for the recess in the upper boundary wall of the fields at 075038. Enter the field to the north and then proceed west down to the huge tips and former entrance of the Bwllfa level. The level entered the hillside on the outcrop of the Rhondda No. 2 seam.

Apart from the water movement within the variable rock sequences, already described on page 25, consider for a moment the water movement

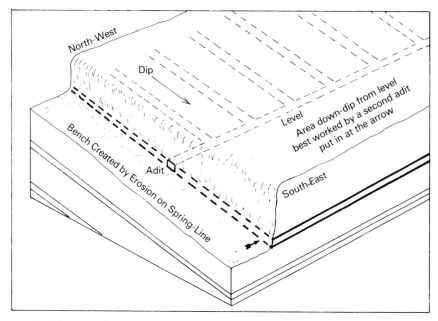

26 The most advantageous arrangement of a level in relation to the dip of the rocks

to be taken into account in the underground workings, movements associated with the SSE dip of the rocks. A level is not just an access route to coal, it inevitably becomes a major water drainage route and the direction in which it is dug will determine its role in this respect, its effectiveness or otherwise in getting rid of the underground water. For example, if the Bwllfa level was driven to the north, up dip, it would act as a natural drainage outlet, helping to de-water the working areas. The coal trams would also have a natural gravity run to the level mouth. If, however, it was driven to the south-east, down dip, it would lose both these advantages. Full trams would need haulage to bring them to the entrance and water would require pumping out, or, to encourage it to go naturally away down dip, another adit would need to be put in, some way further south along the hillside.

Until a year or so ago, the Bwllfa level still had a fine headgear of winding drums at its then open entrance, also serving the incline plane below. Standing in front of the level, the big cone-like dumps run to the right, the furthest being mainly of burnt shale indicating steam engine power or, possibly, coking activity, while the one to the left is of normal Coal Measure waste. Straight ahead a fine incline plane, served no doubt by the former winding gear, leads down to the South Duffryn colliery site and this can be followed down to Dyffryn and from there to the old A470, and so south to regain the starting point of this walk. On the way down more crop workings are passed and a small early waste dump from one of them borders the south side of the incline.

5. Western valley-side above Troedyrhiw

The walk begins at the top of Cwm Du road by the junction with Diana Street, 06800205. Follow the lane which passes up under the new viaduct of the A470 dual carriageway. The lane ascends the Nant Cwm-du valley. Notice how the stream has been channelled under the viaduct to prevent bank erosion around the piers and abutments. The piers are founded in a Pennant sandstone bed which can be seen behind the house on the south side. Beyond the viaduct, pass the chalet bungalow on the right and, at the entrance to the drive of another bungalow on the left, turn up the steep grassy track into the fields above. Cross the stile after noting the pits of old crop workings on the Rhondda No. 1 coal seam. Like many crop workings, these may date from the time of a miners strike. Once over the stile, aim left of the scattered oak trees, to pass uphill beneath the electricity transmission lines. Just south of the most solitary oak tree there is another line of crop workings, marking the outcrop of the No. 1 Rhondda Rider seam. The largest of these, immediately south of the oak tree, is the old Berry No. 1 level, where 4 m of sandstones overlying the coal are still exposed. The entrance to the level beneath is still just open and inside it two of the colliery support arches can be seen. Do not attempt to enter.

From this spot there is a good view northwards over Nant Cwm-du to the waste tips of the old Castle Colliery. The shaft was further north beyond the

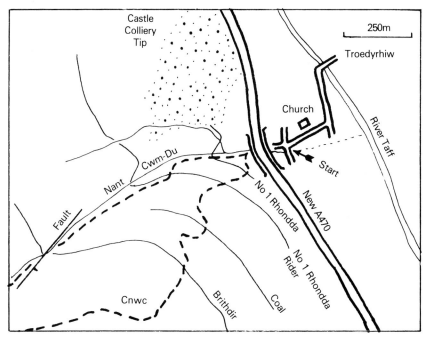

27   Route of the walk west of Troedyrhiw

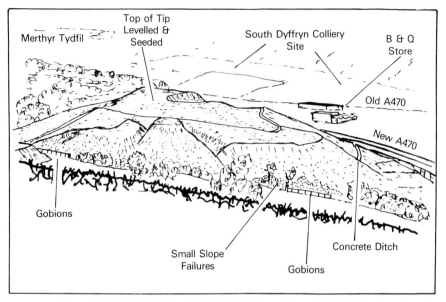

28   Castle Colliery tip from the northeast slopes of Cnwc

tips. These tips have represented a potential threat to the housing estate below, a problem increased by the construction of the new dual carriageway across the toe of the dumps, and several measures have been taken to prevent a slope failure from threatening either roadway or homes. These can be seen from this vantage point or as one continues to climb up the slopes above.

Notice the small slope failures at the base of the near faces of the tip and the stone-filled gobions to contain any slumping which may occur. To the top left there are more gobions, lining the bank of a small tributary of the Nant Cwm-du where it cuts across the SW corner of the dumps. The top of the dump has been levelled and reseeded; a vegetation cover is essential in helping to stabilise a tip and prevent surface gullying. On the slopes facing the main Taff valley, two surface water drainage ditches have been constructed for the same reason, the prevention of gullying.

Resume the climb towards the summit of Cnwc. Use the zig-zag path which rises over the outcrops of Rhondda Beds sandstones and passes over two more lines of crop workings. These lie on a thin coal, possibly the Tyla Court, and on the Brithdir seam. The pits of the crop workings on the Brithdir seam are the larger. Beyond them the final rise to the summit is in thin, cross-bedded, flaggy sandstones. Numerous blocks, some *in situ*, others not, are scattered around the summit and from the hill-top there is a fantastic view up and down the Taff valley, taking in almost the whole area covered by the three volumes in this series. Incidentally, the thin flaggy beds of the hill-top were once quarried for roofing tiles. These were the original roofing materials of the valleys farmhouses, used before railways or canals made possible the import of the so-called traditional North Wales slates. A few cottages still have these flagstone roofs, e.g., at Rhyd y Car, near the start of walk 3. To the north the view extends up to the summits of the Beacons and the Old Red Sandstone country. The dip-slopes of the Carboniferous Limestone and the Millstone Grit are prominent, sloping southwards towards the observer. Note again the difference in the heights of Cefn Cil-Sanws and Pemmoelallt, described in walk 3.

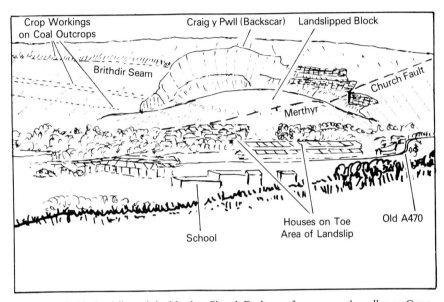

29 Troedyrhiw landslip and the Merthyr Church Fault seen from across the valley on Cnwc

The slopes across the valley, visited on the previous walk, 4, can now be seen in plan. Those who have done that walk, and now recovered their breath here on the top of Cnwc, will agree that the one opposite is the steeper of the two. This is for good geological reasons. On the east side of the valley the dip of the beds is slightly into the ridge and there is less tendency for tributary streams and springs to emerge and erode the hillside than here on the western slopes where the dip is out of the ridge, i.e., converging towards the Taff. There are more tributaries, like the Nant Cwm-du, strong lines of springs, and, just to the south above Aberfan, the results can be seen for the slopes have been worn back into a broad embayment.

Looking across to the east side again, notice the displacement in level of the lines of crop workings on either side of the Troedyrhiw landslip. This is the effect of the Merthyr Church Fault made visible. The full height of Craig y Pwll, the backscar cliff of the landslip, can also be seen. Look further up and more towards the SE to Penddeugae Fach Farm. To its south there is a large forestry plantation. The Cefn Glas seam, described in

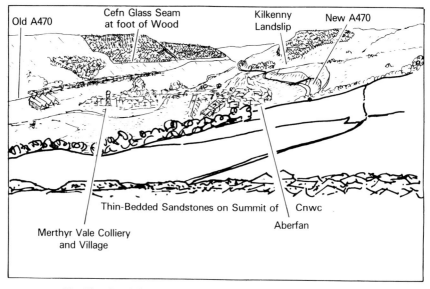

Labels on figure:
Old A470 | Cefn Glass Seam at foot of Wood | Kilkenny Landslip | New A470
Thin-Bedded Sandstones on Summit of | Cnwc
Merthyr Vale Colliery and Village | Aberfan

30   View South from summit of Cnwc to Aberfan and Merthyr Vale

Volume One, outcrops along the lower edge of this wood and there were several old levels dug along there. However, their tips have now been regraded. A road follows the outcrop south to join the old A470 beyond Mount Pleasant, (see walk 6, below).

Below Cnwc the new A470 dual carriageway climbs the hillside to skirt behind Aberfan, and in doing so it has required a special cutting through sandstones of the Upper Coal Measure Brithdir Beds. The engineering of the road is described in more detail later, but from this viewpoint the vertical face created in the sandstones can be seen by the bridge which crosses the main road and, above the cutting, the many surface water drainage and control measures which were required to prevent the drift cover above from slipping over into the roadway. It is apallingly ironic to think that, had the road been built first—and in the light of present day geological knowledge of the problems such virtually instantaneous man-made erosion can cause, and the solutions necessary—then the Aberfan tip would have been dealt with effectively (just like that of the Castle Colliery to the north). The awful tragedy of 1967 would never have occurred. Great lessons are often learned from great tragedies and this has certainly been the case since the Aberfan disaster. The lives which were so cruelly taken then may well have saved others from potentially similar fates.

The head gear of the Merthyr Vale colliery stands among the buildings of the villages 260 m (850 ft) below our vantage point here on Cnwc. Located between and hemmed in by Aberfan and Merthyr Vale, its shaft commences in the Rhondda Beds and first penetrates a surprising 113 m (374 ft) of drift. Since the shaft head here is at 135 m (442 ft) above sea level, this means that the solid rock base of the valley is only 22 m above it, an indication of the enormous overdeepening and gouging which occurred during the Ice Age. In the solid rocks below, the shaft penetrated seams as follows:

		metres	*feet*
No. 2 Rhondda	at minus	36	119
Two Feet Nine	,,	242	794
Four Feet	,,	256	841
Six Feet	,,	271	891
Nine Feet	,,	305	1001
Yard	,,	333	1093
Seven Feet	,,	342	1123
Five Feet and Gellideg	,,	357	1172

Years ago, the main consideration of coal owners faced with the problems of mine waste was the cost of dumping it. Here, with the pit villages crowded closely around the colliery, the steep and impossible slopes of the eastern valley-side, and the need not to obstruct the river along the valley bottom, the longer gentler slope up to the west became the inevitable and ultimately disastrous choice.

Preparatory drainage measures under such a large tip complex would have been negligible in its original days, and so it spread up over a time bomb, the numerous spring-lines which normally emerge from a Coal Measure succession. The great need in tip safety is the control of water movement and pressure within the tip, and if this is not checked then a build up occurs to the point where the water pressure in all the pores between the material becomes high enough to force the waste rock particles out of contact with each other. The whole mass is then 'unlocked' as it were; effectively it becomes a fluid body and capable of flow failure.

The Tyla Court, Brithdir and Brithdir Rider seams all outcrop across the area covered by the former tip and, directly above it, the outcrop of the Cefn Glas seam, previously noted on the eastern valley-side, returns up the western slopes. Passing just above the head of the former tip, this seam is noted for the strong spring line associated with it.

Walk westwards across the summit of Cnwc but take care not to jam a leg in the deep open joints which have formed on its surface. These are due to cambering, the sandstones of the hill top tilting slightly downwards and outwards. A natural process for an isolated hill top, this was no doubt accelerated by quarrying on the western side where a 5 m face remains. Near this, one particularly dangerous joint has been partly filled in by tipping a large flat sandstone slab into it.

West of the small quarry face is a fenced-off holding reservoir, constructed with other drainage measures visible to the west to control the relocated Aberfan tip debris which now sits on the higher slopes beyond. There is water in the reservoir in winter and spring, and a strong flow in the feeder channel leading into it, but in summer all may be dry. Walk around the enclosure and over to the feeder channel by the little sandstone-bedded

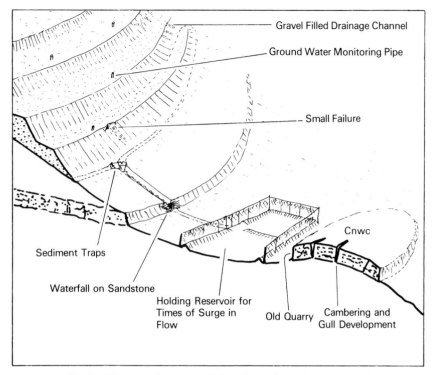

Gravel Filled Drainage Channel

Ground Water Monitoring Pipe

Small Failure

Cnwc

Sediment Traps

Waterfall on Sandstone

Holding Reservoir for Times of Surge in Flow

Old Quarry

Cambering and Gull Development

31 Stability control measures of the re-located Aberfan tip material

waterfall. Notice how the channel above the fall is stepped, to slow and dissipate the water's energy. At the head of that section there are v-notched metal plates which control the ditches entering the systems. They slow the water down on entry too, but their main purpose is as sediment traps, removing rock waste which would otherwise aid erosion of the channel below. Above the sediment traps note the stone-filled cages or gobions which prevent bed erosion of the ditches.

The slope ahead is the lowest of eight terraces of Aberfan tip waste. Walk up it to examine the features of tip control and safety. Samples of coal, fossil plants, and rusty-brown septarian ironstone nodules can be found on the slopes and flats of the complex.

Pipes project about 1 m above the terraces here and there. These are cap boreholes for regularly monitoring the water pressure and movement within the tips. Notice how wet the terrace surfaces remain in wet weather. Most of the flats grade gently west, so that this surface water runs gently back towards the base of the next higher terrace. It is then led away northwards to the edge of the complex, then round and down the ditch leading to the sediment traps already described. The gently graded zig-zag route therefore keeps down its speed and, hence, its erosive power as well. However, saturated conditions can still cause failure and gullies in the terrace faces, and these can be seen from time to time, forming arcuate scars, with the flattened grass below testifying to the water which has flowed from them. Such features must be dealt with before they develop into major gullies. Examples of the measures used can be seen by walking to the northern end of terraces 2, 3 or 4, where large limestone chippings (Carboniferous Limestone) have been used to fill a number of drainage channels. Their even size allows for the passage of water, while restricting its speed, i.e., they keep an open pore system working for some time before fine sediment eventually clogs them and they have to be renewed.

From the northern side of the terraces follow the Nant Cwm-du back towards the start of the walk. Keep close to the wall and the edge of the forestry plantation. Hummocky ground is crossed, a sure sign of natural hillside movement, and this too is monitored by boreholes. Where a track crosses the stream and enters the gate into the forest to the north, also cross the stream but do not go through the gate. Instead, keep close to the fence and continue down valley, scrambling over a deep gully and then carefully descending a jointed and cambered sandstone face. The beds are thin and flaggy, and below them coal levels can be seen just inside the forestry fence. This is the outcrop of the Brithdir seam again. The valley here is marked by a small fault and sandstone crags seen on its southern slopes are thrown down to a slightly lower level.

Below that point, cross the stream and follow a better marked track down its south bank. In the deciduous woods below, the track skirts a large slope-failure area with a flat section by the stream at its base. The failure has occurred over the former entrances to the Berry No. 2 levels which worked on the No. 1 Rhondda Rider seam. The dumps were across the Nant Cwm-du, to the north.

Continue down to the gate and then down the lane back to the starting point of this walk.

6. Mountain road above Merthyr Vale

Drive up the lane which branches off the old A470 road just south of Mount Pleasant at 082983 and runs NNE above Mount Pleasant, Merthyr Vale and Troedyrhiw. This is a real mountain road and drivers should not admire the scenery too much! The lane follows the outcrop of the Cefn Glas seam, along the lower margins of two forestry plantations. Across the valley to the west is the large natural post-glacial landslip associated with the Kilkenny fault and described in Volume One, page 32 and Figure 13. Drive on to the first point where it is convenient to park, where the lane becomes dual track for a few metres by the largest of the former levels on the Cefn Glas seam. Here there is a fine mountain-side vantage point over the works executed to keep the new A470 stable as it skirts the foot of that huge landslip, and also a full-face view of the slopes where the Aberfan tip was located. You can complete your studies in Volume Three and revise Volume One from the same spot!

Looking down valley it is worth mentioning the effect of the new road works on the walk described in Volume One. The route of the walk remains substantially intact and the whole of the outward journey from Quakers' Yard (not visible from this viewpoint) can be followed. The river can still be crossed at Pontygwaith, but beyond the bridge the access under the new dual carriageway is for pedestrians only now, and, ascending the western valley-side, although many of the features described on the return route remain intact, it is best to continue south-westwards up to the regraded tip area to the north of the Giant's Bite. Then proceed south to the Bite and back down to the new cutting where the bridge carries the lane down to Quakers' Yard over the new road. The cutting provides an excellent section in cross-bedded silvery-grey Pennant sandstones.

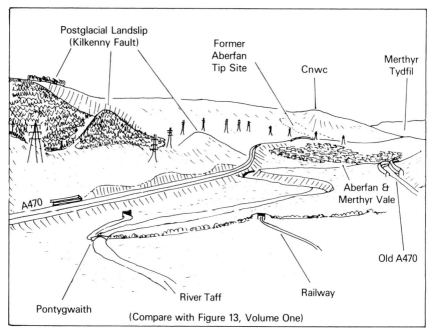

32   The new A470 dual carriageway in relation to the natural landslip South of Aberfan

Turning one's attention back to the view opposite and to the north, the major features of interest are the various measures taken to stabilise the hillsides around the old Kilkenny Fault landslip and in the various new cuttings made for the road as it continues towards Merthyr Tydfil. Unfortunately, when driving the new road, the lay-by provision seldom coincides with the geological interest. The most well-placed one is that on the south-bound carriageway where the plaque to commemorate the opening of the road stands. That is near the foot area of the old landslip, but it is still generally best to see it and the other features with the aid of binoculars from this lane.

A new road represents instantaneous erosion, damage which might take thousands of years by natural processes. Without suitable precautions there would certainly be 'knock-on' effects. Thus, the landslip associated with the Kilkenny Fault was thoroughly investigated prior to the construction of the new road across its lower slopes. Answers were sought as to whether it was still slowly moving? What were the groundwater conditions and pressures within it? Were there any slippery clay layers likely to act as slide surfaces, etc? The fact that a railway and the old Glamorgan Canal had, as described in Volume One, previously crossed it was no reliable guide. Two basic aims had to be secured—a thorough control of the water underground, and an equally thorough management of any water running on the surface. For the former, water pressure must be kept low enough for the rocks to remain in contact, locked together; that is, the water in the spaces between never allowed to pressurise to the point where the rock fragments would be forced apart and behave as if a liquid. Increases in groundwater flow after winter storms had to be known, and safe routes planned for getting the water out.

Similarly, on the surface, water run-off has to be controlled by elaborate systems of drainage ditches and channels, designed to allow it to flow away at reasonable, non-destructive speeds, with concrete collection ditches at the top of each new man-made slope, and broad adits beneath the new embankments to lead it safely down the slopes below.

The River Taff too must not be allowed to swing against the base of the lower slopes, eroding or steepening them, and thus risking the re-activation of the landslip. The river at this point was realigned and concrete retaining walls were built along its banks.

All these measures can be seen from this viewpoint. Beyond them the road rises uphill to pass clear of the village of Aberfan. Another small piece of engineering geology can be seen on its climb northwards—part of the bank has required retention by stone-filled gobions, and by black netting to stabilise the top soil while vegetation is encouraged to re-colonise the bank.

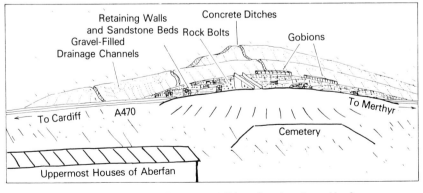

33 Stability measures in the new A470 road cutting above Aberfan

49

Concrete surface-water ditches bound the upper side of all the excavations as you look further north to the major cutting above Aberfan. Here there are measures both to hold firm the Brithdir sandstones (Upper Coal Measures) which form the face of the cut and to stabilise the drift cover on the slopes above. The sandstones have been dealt with by the use of rock bolts whose heads and plates are particularly seen beneath the bridge, and by building retaining walls wherever the natural rock bed seemed unreliable. The drift beds above are controlled by numerous gravel-filled parallel drainage channels, or, in other cases some arranged like the outlines of trees, and also by concrete ditches. Plenty of surface water runs off the hillsides here and the Six-Inch geological survey map particularly notes the strong line of springs issuing close to the outcrop of the Cefn Glas seam at the top of the slopes to the west.

Other features further north cannot be seen from this vantage point and are best viewed when using the road, preferably as a passenger. The next cutting north of the one above Aberfan is on the ridge below Cnwc, the drainage divide between the Taff's Nant-y-maen and Nant Cwm-du tributaries. This is a smaller cutting, created in measures between the No. 1 Rhondda and the No. 1 Rhondda Rider seams. It reveals cross-bedded Pennant sandstones with broad channel features and two thin coals. Beyond it a viaduct takes the road over Nant Cwm-du and the start of the previous walk described. Lastly, as the road approaches the roundabout where the present construction ends, the banks on its west are again stabilised by gravel-filled ditches, and a rock-fall terrace half way up the slope. The latter is designed to catch any small failures above, preventing immediate threat to the carriageways below.

For those who are enjoying the mountain views from this lane north of Merthyr Vale however, and who are willing to leave the details of the new main road until later on, continue up the lane past Penddeugae Farm. About 0.5 km beyond the cattle grid on the open moor to the north, a small fault scarp developed across the road in 1983. Anyone driving over it would have certainly noticed it! A drop of 45 cm developed! The fault ran diagonally across the road, NW-SE, on the trend common to the majority of the coalfield's faults, and with its downthrown side towards the northeast. Traffic avoided it by taking to the grass and it was later filled with light grey Dowlais slag, but it has since moved again and can still be easily located, as can the small fault scar in the pasture on either side. The fault was most likely the result of mining subsidence within the ridge below and, although it follows the same trend, it is not aligned with any of the better-known local faults.

If the explorer continues up the road northwards, the top part of walk 4 can be joined, the cross-bedded sandstones of the ridge top where hang glider flying is so popular. The road then continues past the Merthyr Tydfil waste disposal site and eventually joins the by-pass about midway between the Hoover factory and Dowlais Top roundabout.

Acknowledgements

Figures 16, 17, 19, 22 and 27 are derived from published 1 : 10,560 Geological Survey maps with the permission of The Director, British Geological Survey.

References

1853 Thomas, Rowland (Idris Ddu)
"Traethawd ar gawg mwnawl Deheudir Cymru." Private publication.

1974 Evans, D. Emlyn. 'More than Just Looking' *Amgueddfa* Vol. 17, 25-28

1979 Gillham, M.; Perkins, J.; and Thomas, C.
Historic Taff Valley, Quakers' Yard to Aberfan
Merthyr Tydfil & District Naturalists' Society.

1980 Perkins, J.W. (*Ed.*)
Cliff & Slope Stability, South Wales
Department of Extra Mural Studies, University College, Cardiff.

1980 Conway, B.W.; Forster, A.; Northmore, K.; and Barclay, W.J.
South Wales Coalfield, Landslips Survey Report EG 80/4.
Special Surveys Division, Engineering Geology Unit,
Institute of Geological Sciences.

1981 Merthyr Teachers Centre Group
Merthyr Tydfil, A Valley Community
D. Brown & Sons Cowbridge.

1982 Perkins, J.; Evans, J.; and Gillham, M.
The Historic Tâf Valleys, Volume 2,
In the Brecon Beacons National Park.
Merthyr Tydfil & District Naturalists' Society.

Part Two:
Social and Industrial History

CLIVE THOMAS

Introduction

Merthyr Tydfil, once the most important of Welsh industrial towns has little
now for the visitor, or native for that matter, which might be considered
tangible reminders of its far famed industrial past.

Only experts now can interpret the remains to be found at the sites of the
old ironworks. Except for the spoil heaps there is little evidence of coal or
ironstone having been mined in the area and what remains of a network of
canals, tramroads and railways diminishes with each passing year.

The clearance of what were seen by many as industrial eyesores
accelerated in the late 1960's and buildings which had stood fifty years or
more after they had ended their working lives disappeared overnight—many
of them unrecorded.

Hand in hand with the indiscriminate clearance of industrial buildings
has gone the redevelopment of the town itself and as well as the wholesale
demolition of areas like Caedraw, Caepantywyll and Georgetown (which
perhaps few would dispute as being undesirable), there has also been the
more questionable removal of smaller areas of housing like the Triangle and
Rhydycar Cottages. Thankfully six cottages from Rhydycar have been
preserved at St. Fagans, but are still nevertheless a loss to our own area and
would have been more meaningful if they had remained as part of an
industrial museum in the town itself.

In the last fifteen to twenty years great interest has been shown in the
history of the town. This has been promoted by schools and societies and
has resulted in the production of numerous pamphlets and books, many
understandably concentrating on the town's industrial development. It
seems a little ironic that it is precisely when the most interest has been
generated that the final eradication of Merthyr's industrial landmarks
should take place.

This section of our book is not yet another attempt to retell the already
well recorded history of nineteenth century Merthyr Tydfil. It is I hope, an
effort through a series of walks, to visit particular areas of interest, and with
the aid of maps and photographs make some sense of what little remains.

The first three of our excursions start at the car park of the College of
Technology and explore an area, much of which was the mineral taking of

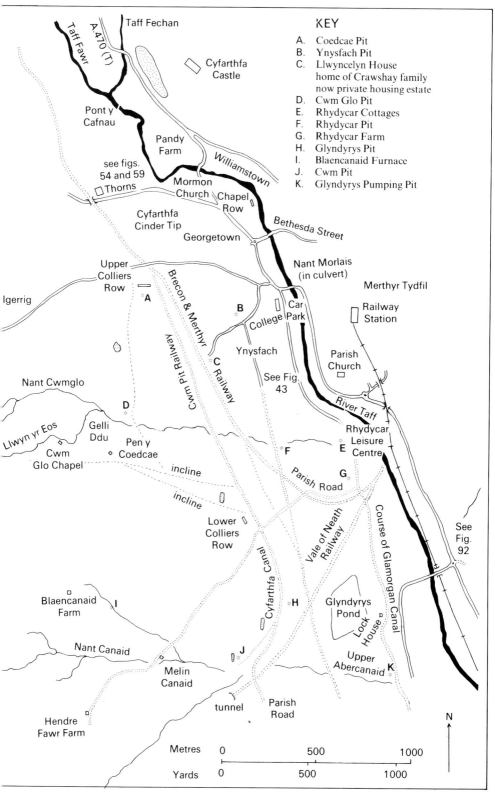

34 Map of Town Area showing areas mentioned in text

the Cyfarthfa Iron Company. They traverse the banks of the River Taff between Cefn Coed and Troedyrhiw, taking the walker onto the hillside overlooking Merthyr Tydfil and offer some spectacular views of the Brecon Beacons to the north and the river valley to the south.

This is of course an ideal spot to begin because the area of the car park was once crossed by the Glamorgan Canal while the College itself occupies the site of the Ynysfach Ironworks, a subsidiary of the Cyfarthfa complex.

But before we move off and follow one or other of our intended walks it is perhaps worth pausing for a moment to contemplate some of the changes which have taken place in our immediate surroundings. This of course is not easily done, as modern concrete-built shops and offices contrast sharply with what many old photographs show, and descriptions tell us, of this area 100 to 150 years ago.

Caedraw and Ynysgau

The Taff itself, although not as aesthetically pleasing at this point as many would like to see it, now more closely resembles the river so highly regarded by many visitors of pre-industrial times than that described by Dr. Dyke in 1850:-

"The water not taken up by the Cyfarthfa Company flows in a deep bed near the works, skirts Caepantywyll, the Cellars, Pontystorehouse, on the lefthand and Georgetown and Ynysfach on the right till it reaches the ironbridge at Merthyr. In this part of its course it receives the contents of some privies on its banks and much of the ashes and refuse from houses is thrown into it.

At the ironbridge, the Ynysfach brook, loaded with sewage from the Georgetown sewer, and with water from the canal, comes into the Taff on the right hand side, on the left it receives the black filthy Morlais."

This brook which rises on the hills above Dowlais was used by both Dowlais and Penydarren ironworks as well as receiving the "sewage from such sewers as there are in Dowlais."

At Pontmorlais at the top of Merthyr High Street "It is further charged by human odure from neighbouring privies, by excretions of the adjacent populace, by refuse from the houses, by the ashes from many houses at some distance off, well prepared with their usual accompaniments of faeces and urine. It continues to receive additional charges of such filth in the remainder of its happily short course, and rolls a heavy black and filthy stream into the Taff.

The united streams now forming the Taff pass under the ironbridge, receive here another charge of ashes and refuse and are weired about 150 yards below the bridge, in order that the water may be conveyed by 'the pond' to the Plymouth ironworks."

Thankfully, the river no longer has to carry away the filth and effluent of

35 The Parish Church and Royal Oak, Caedraw showing the Merthyr Fountain on its original site

ironworks and town, its waters littered now by only the occasional car tyre and supermarket trolley.

Looking first to the south across the weir we can see the modern flats of Caedraw which were built in the 1960's to replace the congested nineteenth century housing. The area's name however, suggests its more rural origins when it was indeed the field outside or beyond the village of Merthyr Tydfil (cae—field; draw—beyond or over there).

Maps of the 1870's show Caedraw bordered by the river and the Plymouth Feeder (known locally as the 'the pond') to consist of Picton Street, its main thoroughfare, and a number of small cross streets, as well as several courts and alleyways with such strangely evocative names as Isle of Wight, Badger's, Currier's and Adam and Eve Courts.

The Ordnance Survey of 1873 shows this small area of Merthyr Tydfil, whose modern boundaries could be taken as the river, Swan Street and the lane behind the Caedraw Schools, as also boasting a tannery, woollen mill, slaughter houses, limekilns, several smithies, a dozen or so public houses, a gas works built in 1836 and even a Turkish baths.

Such maps help us with location, furnish us with a framework for the town and even indicate more specifically trades and occupations carried on in certain areas. It is however, the writings of those who visited or lived in these areas which paint the vivid, sometimes horrific pictures of what life was like in the houses of Caedraw and the other streets which were built along the banks of the River Taff.

A correspondent of the 'Morning Chronicle' writing in 1849 said that:-
"The first impression of a stranger who visits Merthyr is that it is a town of workmen's houses.

The style of building is of the rudest and least commodious kind . . . there still exist (in the lower town—still called the 'village') several of the original houses, mere hovels of stone having no upper storey, and covered with thatch, the eaves of which may be touched with the hand".

With the rapid influx of people from many different parts of the British Isles these already inadequate dwellings inevitably became overcrowded. The Census of 1851 shows that many became lodging houses, those in the Isle of Wight area attracting mainly Irish immigrants. One house in Currier's Row was occupied by John Gleeson, his wife, two sons and eight lodgers whilst next door, the Canes, a family of six from Waterford shared their house with six lodgers, three of whom hailed from Sligo and were described as bone gatherers.

Such houses, no doubt resembled those visited by the 'Morning Chronicle' reporter a year or so earlier. He found one lodging house in Caedraw where "the floor was broken and unwashed, and the rooms stinking and filthy in the last degree. The price of beds was from 2d. to 4d. a night. We here saw a stout Irish woman, barefooted, in a blue cloak, with one child on her back and five around her".

Nearby in another four roomed house the reporter counted sixteen persons in two downstairs rooms but was refused permission to inspect the upper rooms.

Already by this time, a settlement of some 40,000 inhabitants, Merthyr had no public sewers or drains and no supply of piped water. It is little wonder that the town was as a consequence frequently visited by epidemics of scarlet fever, typhoid and cholera.

All these diseases were of course greatly encouraged by hunger, dirt and overcrowding but while typhus was carried in the faeces of lice which dries to a light powder and infects through inhalation or via cuts, cholera, a highly infectious disease which attacked the intestines, was carried in polluted water and by flies contaminating food. This was not appreciated at the time, many people thinking it some form of invisible gas which mysteriously attacked its victims.

Although speaking figuratively about such a visitation of cholera, Sir William Kay perhaps epitomises the fear and despair the disease engendered in the town population,

"It may hover over a town, but unless attracted by local causes, it passes by, a passive and inocuous wanderer, despoiled of its prey and impotent for mischief.

Like the thunder cloud of summer it may lour and threaten; distant mutterings and a darkened horizon attesting its latent and destructive capabilities; but cleanliness, like the lightening rod, neutralizes its powers and averts the impending attack".

Evidence given to an enquiry opened by T. W. Rammell in May 1849, tragically catalogues the deplorable conditions which existed in the town and were responsible for an epidemic of cholera which broke out at the end of that month and continued into September. In those months over 1400 people died of the disease.

Although not the poorest part of town, it is obvious that the dual problems of water supply and sewage disposal affected Caedraw as much as any other part of Merthyr Tydfil. Mr. William Harris in evidence to the enquiry stated:-

"I obtain my supply of water for drinking from the Caedraw pump—it is a private pump—and pay 6d. a quarter for the use of it. The water of the pump is not so good as the spring on the other side of the river. The pump water is harder and does not draw the strength out so much as soft water. The servant girls sent after water often dally their time out, and stay there times as long as necessary for them. People in my opinion go to the spring in preference to the pump, not to save 6d. a quarter so much as to get a better water. The peculiar character of the water is, that it deposits a great sediment when boiled: I believe it affects the health of the people drinking it, and my own health in particular. It caused indigestion, and a pain in the back in the region of the kidney's".

I am unable to discover the precise location of the spring referred to but what is evident is the only means the servant girls had of carrying the water from the other side of the river was across the stepping stones, as no bridge existed along this stretch of river in those days.

Mr. Harris goes on to describe water from another spring nearby, perhaps 100 yards from the Parish burial ground in Twynyrodyn:-

"When this water is kept twenty-four hours it is impossible to drink it, on account of its offensive smell, which I can compare to nothing else than that arising from decayed animal matter. I believe that is communicated to the water from it being surface water passing though the burial ground. There are privies and cesspits on the side of the hill above the springs and these may also affect the water."

The large slaughterhouse in Caedraw also contributed to the general problem as the "blood and refuse of the animals is washed into the pond". In a postscript on the epidemic of 1849, written in December of that year, Dr. T. J. Dyke stated:-

"Many of the cases of cholera occured in Mill and Pond Streets, which are close to the parish church burial ground. There are ten houses built with their backs to the churchyard, in seven of them there were to my knowledge, nine cases of cholera and diarrhoea. Interments took place here also, though the yard was previously replete with the remains of the dead".

The Local Board of Health, set up in 1850, was given powers to lay down a sewerage system and provide an adequate water supply but it was not until 1858 that the work of supplying the water began and 1861 before it was actually available from standpipes in the streets. The changes brought about by these basic improvements should not however, be underestimated, and the implications it seems were wide ranging as far as Caedraw was concerned. By 1870 not only did many of the houses have their own piped water supply but 'the village' sported its very own Turkish Baths. Perhaps not of the standard of those Grecian edifices described by Seneca where the waters were conveyed through silver pipes and the walls were laboriously stuccoed in imitations of painting, the baths at Caedraw were nevertheless impressive by local standards.

"The visitor is ushered into a well appointed and snugly carpeted reception room to the left of the chief entrance. On the right is a spacious cooling room, furnished with divans of velvet upholstery, on which the bathers lie after their bath, and by just touching the electric bell push overhead an attendant is summoned, and refreshments may be ordered according to the visitors own peculiar taste.

In this room there are likewise a range of dressing compartments of conspicuous eastern aspect; in fact the whole compartment is imbued with eastern notions. Emerging from the cooling room one enters hotroom No. 1

36   The Turkish Baths at Plymouth Street, about 1910   *M.B.C.*

admirably appointed and fitted with electric bells and other accessories, and registering 140 degrees of heat. Those aspirants who prefer it a little warmer may step into hotroom No. 2, where 200 degrees of heat are registered. In the ordinary course of things, the shampooing room will next claim attention where by scientific manipulation at the hands of a trained masseur, every nerve and muscle of the human frame is restored to its natural action and elasticity.

Bidding adieu to the reception and cooling rooms, the next object of interest is the swimming bath, a lofty, spacious apartment, well lighted by an excellent arrangement of skylights, the bath itself being thirty-six feet in length and twenty-five feet in breadth—having a shelving, sloping bottom so that the risk of mishaps to bathers is reduced to a minimum. Above the bath is an aquatic trapeze, and swinging apparatus, by means of which useful appliances the swimmer may disport and launch himself with ease into shallow or deeper water, as he may desire. In winter the water is run off, and the bath is turned into a gymnasium for boxing, fencing and athletic exercises generally''.

Directly across the River Taff from the college car park, Ynygau Chapel stood to the right of the traffic lights at the bottom end of Castle Street and another Merthyr landmark, Watkyn George's cast iron bridge spanned the river at this point. A study of the two photographs Figures 37 and 38 shows

37 Ynysgau. The railings of the chapel can be seen on the right and in the distance is the archway which led into Castle Street   *M.B.C.*

59

38 The archway was near to where the traffic lights are now at the river end of Castle Street
M.B.C.

clearly the changes which have taken place since pubs like the Patriot, Parrot and Iron Bridge Vaults stood in the cluster of buildings around Ynysgau Chapel.

The iron bridge, which was unceremoniously dismantled and dumped in Cyfarthfa Park in 1963, was designed and built by Watkyn George, engineer of the Cyfarthfa Works. It replaced an earlier stone bridge which crossed the river a little further downstream and had collapsed after a long period of frost.

Work on the new bridge began in the middle of 1799 and was completed by May 1800. It became a vital link between the Ynysfach/Georgetown area and the town itself. Spanning sixty-eight feet, the bridge was built in three separate sections with the road surface formed of stone setts.

By the middle of the nineteenth century, concern was being expressed about the condition of the bridge which was becoming dilapidated and dangerous. Superintendent Wren reported to the Local Board of Health in March 1852 that, "I have no hesitation in pronouncing it unsafe for traffic in its present state". It was suggested that a new bridge should be built but this was ignored and it seems that his recommendations at least spurred the authorities to carry out certain repairs. A further survey carried out in 1860 highlighted the bridge's importance as a thoroughfare in terms of the volume of traffic using it. A census carried out between the hours of 8 a.m. and 8 p.m. during the last week of June showed a total 57,716 foot

39 The Merthyr ironbridge with Victoria Street in the background

40 The ironbridge during demolition and showing where stone setts had been removed from the cast iron frame.

passengers, 773 horses, 1881 wheeled vehicles and 507 cattle crossed the bridge. It would be another twenty years however, before a replacement bridge was built. After that the old iron bridge would be used only by pedestrians. On its demolition, a chemical analysis carried out on a sample of the iron contained in the bridge showed nothing unusual in its composition and certainly nothing to support claims of rustless iron.

Although somewhat diminished by recent landscaping this area of town is still dominated by the not inconsiderable bulk of the 'British Tip'. This tip, originally formed by the waste from the Penydarren Ironworks affords an excellent panorama of the surrounding area, its elevated character of course, being used to good effect by the rioters of 1831, for it was from here that they fired on the Highland troops stationed in and around the Castle Inn (the site of cinema and bingo hall).

Later, in the early 1860's the flattened top of the tip was taken as the site of the British and Foreign Schools Society's Abermorlais Schools. Three separate schools, boys, girls and infants occupied an impressive two-storeyed building which was demolished in 1972. Although by then run-down, the building was still a fine example of mid-Victorian school architecture with external walls still bearing faded maps of the Empire which had once been used for outdoor lessons, and slogans imploring children to keep the playground tidy by putting banana skins in the waste bin.

The headteacher's school log book provides a colourful and valuable insight into those early years of universal education. Many involved with modern education practise might be horrified to read of some of the conditions which prevailed in these buildings (although some contemporary structures still exist) but sobered and, maybe, reassured to find that there are also many aspects of school life which appear eternal. The headteacher, then as now was bothered by recalcitrant pupils and idiosyncratic teachers alike, whilst the apprehension with which an impending visit from one of Her Majesty's Inspectors was viewed has perhaps moderated only slightly. The following are extracts from the log of the boys' school:—

Abermorlais Boys School was opened as a British School on *April, 20th. 1868.* With Mr. E. Jones as Headmaster.

May 4th. 1868. Third week of school being opened, 217 boys admitted up to this day but many of them left, the majority having only come for the first three days when no school fees were exacted.

Thursday, December 7th. 1870. Came into school this day about 1.30 p.m., the dinner hour and found I had no teacher in charge. On enquiring I learnt that it was Mr. Jenkins, Abercanaid week. At 1.45 p.m. Wm. Lloyd came to school and asked if he could ring the bell. I gave him consent to do so. At eight minutes to two Wm. Jenkins came in. On asking him how he had not had charge of school he said he had arranged with Wm. Jenkins, Penyrheol and Wm. Lloyd to take charge of it in his absence. I told him that I could not hold them responsible for his week. After some conversation he said that he would rather leave than eat his dinner in school. I told him he may do as he liked about leaving but that he must abide by my rules whilst he was in school.

April, 30th, 1871. From the Inspector's annual report. . . . "The practice of 'tipping' all the town refuse just outside the playground should be dealt with under the nuisance removal act.

Jan. 1st. 1872. Very few children in school, many being away soliciting New Year gifts.

July 1872. Found William Rees the pupil teacher frightening a little boy in his classroom after the other children had left by placing him in a "black hole" which he had constructed out of blackboards. There were other teachers including Jenkin Jenkins the senior pupil teacher present witnessing the punishment of the child without making any effort to prevent it.

February 20th. 1872. Mr. Waddington H.M.I. paid a "visit of surprise". He came in about ten minutes before four and examined the timetable.

The inspector found that the timetable was not being adhered to and objected to this.

He objected to the timetable being departed from in the slightest degree and stated that a repetition of the same circumstances would cause a deduction in the grant. He called for the log book and examined it. He then asked questions as to the professional ability of the several pupil teachers but did not examine their actual teaching.

Friday, March 8th. 1872. Committee meeting to take into consideration the remarks of H.M. Inspector respecting the deviation from the timetable in the Boys school. Managers gave directions that the master should write to the inspector to return the timetable which had been forwarded to him by post for approval.

Wednesday, March 20th. Received timetable from Mr. Waddington, approved.

Tuesday, March 26th. Cautioned Wm. Lewis about punishment he meted out.

April 1872 Establishment consisted of Headmaster, John E. Jones, 1st. Class Certificate and five pupil teachers.

May 15th. 1872. Attendance very low this week again. There are 25 absent this week on account of small pox.

May, 22nd. Found Wm. Jenkins, first year pupil teacher, reading novels in class. Censured him and explained to him the nature of the offence he was committing.

May, 24th. Wm. Jenkins absent this day without leave. His absence causes considerable inconvenience as there was no one to mark his register.

Friday, September 6th. 1872. O. Reakes took charge of the school on Monday. Found the school room in a very dirty state and the appearance and habits of the children to correspond. The supply of reading books and slates is ample.

Sept. 9th. Wm. Rees, Wm. Lloyd and Wm. Jenkins absent from pupil teacher classes without leave.

I find that the second year pupil teachers are very much behind in their homework. Wm. Lloyd is especially ignorant.

Sept. 30th. Find that many boys have left and gone to the new board school which opened this morning. Commenced night school with 75 boys.

October, 31st. The writing of William Rees' class is very bad and the teacher very careless.

November, 25th. 1872. Wm. Jenkins (first Year Pupil Teacher) rang the school bell on Saturday for mischief. Had to warn William Rees about striking boys.

December 3rd. Have sent to Mr. Williams the builder to repair the chain on the bell for the 12th. time.

1873.

January 6th. Found William Jenkins' class in disorder and the teacher quietly eating nuts.

February, 3rd. Few children at school this morning owing to the cold and the heavy fall of snow. As no fires were lit at 9 o'clock we took drill instead of the subjects mentioned in the timetable. William Rees (Third Year Pupil Teacher) not brought in his homework.

February 4th. The home lessons of William Rees not learnt, the excuse he has given is that he had no time, owing to the science class.

February, 5th. Jenkin Jenkins pupil teacher having obtained a First Class Queen's Scholarship left for Borough Road Training College: the master presented him, in the name of the scholars and teachers of a portmanteau and dressing case, as a token of their esteem.

February, 24th. A very heavy fall of snow in the night which has continued through the day, the attendance has been low in consequence.

February, 25th. Attendance improved, though the weather very cold. Found about four boys snowballing on the tip with some of the teachers leading them.

February, 26th. Had two complaints of boys being ill used by teachers.

March 3rd. Kept the whole school after school hours this afternoon for disorder.

March, 11th. William Rees' homework was very carefully done last night.

March, 19th. At 2 o'clock the lads belonging to this school were stopped at the foot of the tips by the boys of St. David's School and a fight with snowballs took place. All the boys not in school at 2 p.m. were kept till 5 p.m.

April, 23rd. In the afternoon I found William Jenkins and William Rees playing in the school room, the latter threw a bottle of red ink.

June 24th. William Lloyd's class has been in disorder for most of the morning.

August, 11th. Reopened school with a very fair attendance. Forty-two panes of glass have been broken during the holidays.

41 & 42   Abermorlais School and its foundation stone. After the death of Sir John Guest, Lady Charlotte remarried Mr. Charles Schreiber

September, 17th. William Lloyd's home lessons not done last night. Sent for his mother who promised to keep him, if possible, to his studies in the evening.

October, 7th. Received another complaint of the striking of boys by Lloyd; as complaints of this kind are frequently made I have thought it my duty to prevent him from teaching until the matter has been brought before the managers.

October, 10th. Sent William Lloyd for the absentees of the week but find that he took a walk to Abercanaid instead.

November, 10th. William Lloyd who has been absent since last Tuesday owing to a black eye returned to school.

1874.

March, 25th. Find a great difficulty in working the school. William Jones is still ill at home and I have six classes quite full and only three young pupil teachers.

July 28th. Found William Lloyd had punished eight boys of the third class by striking them on the head with a cane, although he has been frequently forbidden to do so.

August, 5th. William Lloyd has gone to a cricket match at Aberdare this afternoon without leave.

September, 25th. William Lloyd has been more careless than usual; his supervision as curator of the school during the dinner hour has been entirely neglected, the consequence is that the ink has been spilt over the desks and other damage done.

September, 29th. Changed today the time for taking the pupil teachers: instead of from seven to eight from twelve to one. No home lesson brought in by William Lloyd who says he was in the Drill Hall.

September 30th. William Lloyd's home lesson not done last night; his reason is that William Jenkins forgot to tell him what to do.

October, 30th. Found that William Lloyd had left his class. His boys were shouting loud enough to be heard throughout the building.

December, 3rd. I find that William Lloyd frequently sends boys on errands for him into the town: he did so this morning though he has been forbidden to do so. A few days ago he sent a boy to the G.W.R. refreshment room for ham and bread at 11 o'clock.

The report of Mr. Waddington H.M.I. for the year ending 31st. December 1874 states that "I am much pleased with the school" the tone and discipline being good. However, he notes that William Lloyd has again failed his examination (despite him claiming illness during exams). The report also notes abuse of boys and the lack of home lessons. No more is heard of William Lloyd after this date and Mr. C. Reakes terminated his engagement on July 2nd. 1875.

Mr. R. M. John became the new headmaster after that date.

1875.

November, 19th. The pupil teachers failed to produce their home lessons twice during the week and brought no satisfactory reason for the irregularity. Spoke to the same about certain objectionable periodicals which I had happened to find about their cupboards and read by them during their dinner hour. They were charged not to introduce them to school at any time.

1876.

October 20th. On Thursday 19th. inst. another charge of ill-treating a child was preferred against Thomas David Evans by the grandmother of John Treherne. The teacher admitted that he had tied the boy by his arm to the desk in the classroom. The headteacher sent him from the class in his charge to the sixth standard to study with the boys of that class.

The Boy (Thomas David Evans) returned only after apologising for his conduct on November 2nd.

November, 11th. Physiology with Standards 4, 5 and 6. The human skeleton. This was a practical lesson—two human skeletons were before the class—a whole and sections of a whole. The boys were delighted with the lesson and examined the various bones with good results.

1877.

September 21st. Many poor boys have recently been admitted and some of them attend in a filthy state. The teacher of that class was instructed to see that all such children do not enter the school until they have washed their hands and faces.

October, 8th. The headteacher inflicted corporal punishment on eight boys for committing nuisances about the corners of the school instead of utilising the urinals.

October, 24th. A complaint was brought to the headteacher about the bad conduct of two scholars in the street. The headteacher spoke to the whole school for about fifteen minutes at the close—on the importance of good conduct everywhere. The boys were impressed with their duty to be respectful to rich and poor alike—not to call after people—not to provoke poor idiots and drunkards—and not to shout and yell especially near houses and when persons pass—as is the custom of some classes of people in this neighbourhood.

1878.

February, 15th. The woman engaged by the Board washed several children from the lowest class. The appearance of this class has recently greatly improved.

December, 11th. Several boys were caught sliding on the fish pond ice. The headteacher succeeded in persuading some to come to school. The rest were punished in the afternoon. Suggested to the School Board Inspector that the attendance officer be instructed to visit the places resorted to by the boys during the frost.

1879.

October 29th. Mr. Williams, a travelling photographer took portraits of the teachers and scholars.

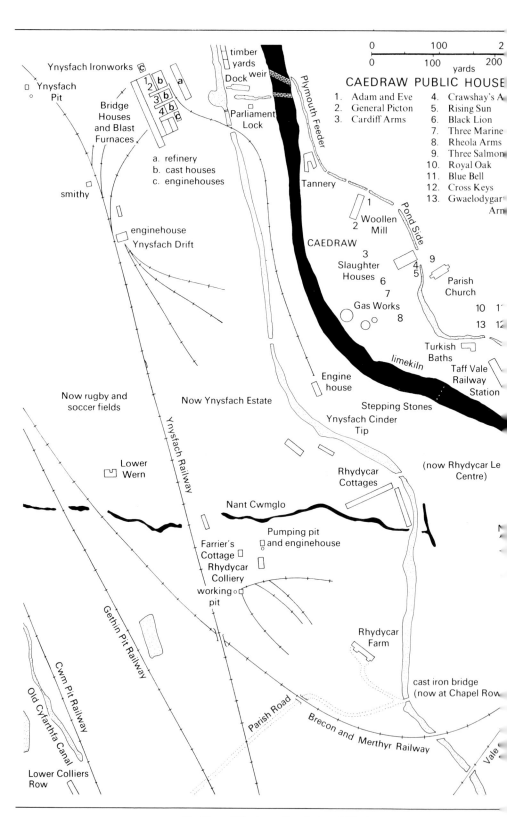

43 Map of Caedraw, Ynysfach and Rhydycar
Based on Ordnance Survey of 1876

1880.
August 25th. Attendance was very good yesterday and today.
August 26th. Attendance was very full. Tickets for the school treat were distributed in the morning. Registers were marked at 9.30 and school dismissed at 11.30. The headteacher and two of the pupil teachers were engaged in making preparation for the school treat at Galon Uchaf Farm.

The school assembled at 1.30 and formed into a procession headed by the Town Brass Band. The procession started at 2.00 p.m. promptly turned down Bethesda Street, went through Dynevor Street, where Georgetown Boys School joined, over the ironbridge, through Victoria and High Streets and Gwaunfarren Road and stopped at Gwaelodygarth House on the way to a field kindly lent by D. Davies Esq. Galon Uchaf.

After tea the children enjoyed themselves by playing at various games provided for them. The 'turn about' was the great attraction to the little ones. The band played all afternoon. The schools returned at eight highly pleased with the days outing. There were 330 boys present.

Ynysfach and Georgetown

The remains of the Ynysfach Ironworks, immediately behind the College of Technology, offer the best opportunity to study an early nineteenth century ironworks. Unfortunately they stand on property which is not always accessible and the furnaces have been partially demolished. The shell of the very impressive blast enginehouse however, has been restored in the last few years and it makes the site well worth a visit.

Four furnaces were built here, the first two and their associated enginehouse in 1801, with the other two and the existing enginehouse being added in 1836. These furnaces once stood over sixteen metres high, but it is the enginehouse now which captures the imagination, typifying as it does the nature of Cyfarthfa architecture and the high degree of skill possessed by its masons. Unlike the main site at Cyfarthfa, where there was a large scale re-modelling of the works in the 1880's, Ynysfach did not make the change over to steel production and consequently the works fell into disuse well before the end of the nineteenth century.

Cast houses, refinery and one of the blast enginehouses have gone, stone from the latter apparently going to construct the fan enginehouse at Lower Gethin Colliery. The furnace tops were removed to make them safe. By the beginning of the century Charles Wilkins found the site already derelict, "the seeds of wild flowers have settled there and germinated. The purple phlox, pimpernel and yellow bedstraw, with great marguerites gather on the top like a crown and even in the dark shadows there lurk infant ferns nigrum and spleenwort".

North along Dynevor Street, the route now takes us past the modern ambulance and fire stations on one side and on the other the Three Horse Shoes, the Kirkhouse Hall and the house once occupied by Judge Joseph Coffin, Clerk to the Court of Requests.

44 Ynysfach Ironworks viewed from the south showing the cast houses of the blast furnaces and the enginehouses. It is of course the building in the distance which still stands

45 Entrance to the cast houses of the first two furnaces to be built at Ynysfach. C. & G. (Crawshay and George) 1801 on keystone

In nineteenth century Merthyr Tydfil, many public houses were often much more than mere drinking places. The Miner's Arms, which occupied the site of the present R.A.F.A. Club, was where in the 1850's and 1860's inquests were held on those who had been killed in the Cyfarthfa mines.

The Three Horse Shoes nearby on the other hand, during the late 1830's and early 1840's, figured prominently as a meeting place for the areas embryonic Chartist movement. In 1838 a Working Man's Association was established in the town, with Morgan Williams, a weaver and moral force chartist from Penyrheolgerrig at its head. The Chartist movement in South Wales generally never recovered from the debacle of the march on Newport in November 1839, but in Merthyr it staged something of a revival in 1842. The group, undoubtedly concerned with redress of local economic grievances, was seen in a more sinister political light by Sir James Graham, the Home Secretary. So seriously in fact were their intentions taken, that by August 1842 agents of the Peel Government were infiltrating their meetings held at the Three Horse Shoes and sending intelligence reports to the Home Office. During late August and September numbers at meetings increased so greatly that open air gatherings were held at Caedraw, Georgetown and Heolgerrig but the leaders continued to meet at the Three Horse Shoes and David Evans' Unitarian schoolroom in Georgetown. Enthusiasm for the Chartist cause seems to have waned soon after, and with only a brief revival in 1848 it suffered complete collapse.

46 Dynevor Street, Georgetown looking north in 1972. All the buildings north of Judge Coffin's house have since been demolished

At the other end of Dynevor Street, the Dynevor Arms was the meeting place for the famous Cyfarthfa Philosophical Society, which re-organised itself in 1855 after being disbanded some years earlier. The society met regularly here for their lectures and discussions.

Dynevor Street has always been busy; the main thoroughfare between the Cyfarthfa environs and the town, it has now become something of a traffic bottleneck. It is certainly difficult nowadays to imagine that Abermorlais School picnic march of 1880 or even more so the scene almost half a century before when a mob marched this way seeking justice and the destruction of the iniquitous Court of Requests. The only house left now in Dynevor Street was once that of Judge Joseph Coffin, Clerk to the court which was principally concerned with the recovery of small debts. The rioters of June 1831 saw the court as an important part of the repression they suffered under, and accordingly sacked the building before turning their anger on the ironmasters themselves, some of whom were in the Castle Hotel. Windows of the house were broken, court records and furniture being thrown into the street and burnt.

Although the riots ended tragically with the shootings outside the Castle Hotel and the hanging of Richard Lewis (Dic Penderyn) one beneficial consequence was the passing of the Anti-truck Act in January 1832. This Act forbade payment of wages in goods and effectively removed the main cause of many of the injustices meted out by the Court of Requests.

Later in the century, on the ground now occupied by the ambulance and fire stations, and situated between river and canal, stood the Taff Vale Brewery. Originally owned by Mr. Thomas Evans, the concern later came into the ownership of David Williams and Co. and much later moved to

47   Taff Vale Brewery Georgetown, showing workers at the turn of the century

that familiar red brick building in Dan y Parc. The brewery at Georgetown, five storeys in height and comprehensive in layout obtained its water from an artesian well on the premises to produce high class pale and bitter ales. The company was awarded a bronze medal at the London Exhibition of 1890 and sold their ales through a large number of public houses which it owned in the Merthyr district.

The brewing industry was well represented in this part of Merthyr for apart from several small breweries associated with individual pubs, at the top of Iron Lane and near to the Corona Soft Drinks garage, was the extensive Cyfarthfa Brewery.

Across the canal from the Taff Vale Brewery was a tannery owned at one time by John Bryant who was High Constable of Merthyr in 1859. Skins from the tanyard were dried in the fields above the present Cyfarthfa Church, before that is, any tipping took place there.

The Kirkhouse Memorial Hall was erected in memory of the Rev. Howell Kirkhouse, one time vicar of Cyfarthfa and member of the family which figured prominently in the exploitation of the Cyfarthfa mineral reserves. The building stands on the site once occupied by the Cyfarthfa National School. The school, built in 1843 to accommodate 300 children was paid for out of deductions from the wages of the Cyfarthfa workmen.

The present Georgetown roundabout was the site of the Glamorgan Canal's first of forty-nine locks. At this point we come to the area once known as Pontystorehouse and across the river at the base of the old cinder tip, the infamous area of Merthyr called 'China'.

Henry Austin Bruce (later Lord Aberdare) once said that Merthyr Tydfil was a town where "no one lived from choice". Whilst this might be regarded as a somewhat exaggerated and unnecessary remark, the same comment might be deemed as having validity when applied to that area of the town whose name became synonymous with poverty, degradation and crime.

To many, the area of Quarry Row and Bethesda Houses was "the abode of filth and a scene of pestilence". The *Morning Chronicle* reporter found a "maze of bleak courts, tortuous lanes and cellars", the conditions he found in them would haunt him to the end of his life:—

"On entering we found three bare-legged women, a man and some children, squatted round the fire. On a string stretched before the fireplace there hung, drying, a quantity of black woollen stockings, almost footless for want of repair. The dimensions of the room were 12 feet by 8 feet, and the only furniture it contained was one rickety three-legged table, a low bench and a log of wood. One of the women ran out and soon returned with a candle, which she lit and carried before us up the ladder, into the loft above. It was not without difficulty we squeezed ourselves through the narrow opening cut through the boards, but having done so we were fairly in the bedroom, the unoccupied space of which we pretty well filled. The cobwebs hung in black films from the roof. On the right and left hand of the entrance were two beds; each might be touched while standing on the ladder. Stooping down with the candle over the bed on the right, the woman pointed to the man—who was in a raging fever. When the doctor had examined him the woman threw up the clothes at the foot of the bed, and showed us a poor child, emaciated from dysentry and from fever, and shivering on its sudden exposure to air. In the room below them lodged two single women and one illegitimate child aged seven years. On what those slept I did not hear; certainly they had no proper bed. The stench of the house was unendurable and we were glad to get away from it.

We next called at the house of an Irishwoman, which though dirty was perhaps less loathesome than we last inspected. The house consisted of two rooms. The first thing we saw on entering was the corpse of a child in a winding sheet, laid out upon a table; a white handkerchief, folded small covered its eyes, but it did not conceal the features, which waxy and pallid, death had composed to a smile. Though the child had been dead two days, it was unprovided with a coffin. The odour of the house was most unsupportable. Before the fire were three or four children; amongst them was a boy named Martin, 11 years of age, which had been placed there by the parish, the allowance being 2s. per week. This boy had no shirt; he was barefooted in rags, his hair bristled up and he was literally black with filth. On looking into the adjoining rooms I saw three beds; two of these were occupied by two married couples, and the third by the children I had seen around the fire''.

If the conditions found in the houses were truly horrendous, those of the streets, particularly in the neighbourhood of one of the many burial grounds, are indeed beyond the bounds of imagination. Mr. Bowie in his evidence to the Rammell inquiry of 1849 describes the area near the Bethesda Chapel burial ground:—

"My attention was directed to this ground, from having seen a number of severe and fatal cases of cholera in the nest of hovels called Bethesda Square, all in a disgusting state of filth. The graveyard is situated above the level of this square, and is itself overtopped especially at the south and east side by an immense heap of refuse and other putrescent matters. There is a well in the square, or rather a hole, containing filthy water, which must necessarily have percolated in part from the graveyard: this water the poor people who came under my notice were only too glad to use when they could obtain it. It is difficult, where so many causes of disease are combined, to ascertain the exact influence of any one cause; but it is my conviction that the state of the churchyard contributes largely to the extraordinary unhealthiness of this spot. Fever is hardly ever absent from it''.

It is little wonder that, offering such a low quality of life, this area became one of last resort for so many and was frequented by the unfortunate and desperate.

Records are often incomplete and accounts perhaps coloured by middle class prejudice but it appears that crime was almost endemic in the

Riverside/Pontystorehouse area. Most of it was undoubtedly petty in character, undertaken by juveniles who lived rough (Superintendent Wren claimed that as many as 150 children were homeless) or had been forced into crime by their parents. In 1846 James Thomas aged 13 was committed as a rogue and a vagabond for stealing a scarf and shawl. He belonged to a gang called the 'Rodnies' which concerned itself mainly with petty theft and pickpocketing. Although a large proportion of these young miscreants were concerned with stealing food to stave off hunger, there was also a more organized aspect to crime in this quarter. Receivers like Richard Mathias (Dick the Thief) and Jenkin Rees were responsible for 'fencing' articles stolen by the younger element.

'Smashers' (coin counterfeiters) were occasionally apprehended in the district whilst the partnership of 'nymph' and 'bully' was one which frequently came to the notice of the courts. Drunks and strangers were lured into China by women whose intent was to rob their clients at the earliest opportunity. Any resistance on the part of the victim was usually overcome by a male accomplice. One such 'bully' who served his apprenticeship with the Rodnies and was later to become one of China's 'Emperors' was John Wylde. In September 1846 this "notorious bully" was charged by P.C. Sterling with rescuing a prisoner from his custody on Saturday night. The constable said that information had been given to him by a sailor that he had been robbed of a waistcoat by one of the 'ladies', whom he took into custody, and when about to convey her to the station, the prisoner and about 100 of the Pontystorehouse inhabitants surrounded him and the prisoner (Wylde) dragged the girl away from him and she escaped. Wylde also said that he would "kick his guts out".

When Superintendent Wren entered the Cellars to take Wylde, "he saw the prisoner standing before his door with a mason's hammer in his hand swearing that he would knock out the brains of the first policeman that came near him". In 1849 Wylde was evidently continuing his colourful career for as a result of being arrested for being drunk and disorderly he managed to smash eleven panes of glass in the police station.

Despite the squalor and degradation which prevailed in this area of town it is somewhat refreshing to note there lived and worked a man who was respected as a philosopher and amateur scientist far beyond the confines of Merthyr Tydfil. Thomas Norbury, originally from Bromsgrove kept an oilshop at Pontystorehouse, above which he constructed an observatory. He was a naturalist, one sympathetic to Darwin's newly expounded theories and a close friend of Rose Mary Crawshay, wife of Robert Thompson Crawshay. Norbury, like Crawshay, is buried in Vaynor Churchyard and his tombstone, albeit less pretentious, tells more of the man than that which marks the ironmaster's grave.

It is at the roundabout, near to Jackson's Bridge, that one is offered the best view of the area which was once occupied by old Grangetown. Now, apart from the buildings of Dynevor Street not a single structure remains to

48 Howell Street, Georgetown ran between John Street and Iron Lane

49 Tramroadside, Georgetown with St. Mary's Church (1971)

give an inkling of what the area looked like. George Street still follows its old line towards Cyfarthfa Church and Heolgerrig although in 1986 it is a street in name only. At this busy road junction the tramway from Ynysfach and Rhydycar crossed, running to the west of the canal before crossing it at the northern end of Chapel Row. John Street and Iron Lane intersected George Street at right angles with Bethel Street running parallel to it. The tramway carried the red haematite ore, which had been brought up the canal from Cardiff, to the Ynysfach Works and was in fact named the Red Mine Tramroad (Y Ddramroad Goch). Along the tramroad, behind Judge Coffin's House, was the old Catholic Church built in 1857 when the Parish of Merthyr, which had been based in Dowlais for many years was divided into two. Immediately in front, on Dynevor Street, and behind in Bethel Street were the Baptist Chapels of Einon and Bethel. Bethel built in 1809 on the flat area of fields known as Yr Ynys pre-dated Einon by almost half a century.

Although varied in character the housing here was some of the best in nineteenth century Merthyr Tydfil. The one up, one down houses of Nanty-gwenith Lane, immediately below Cyfarthfa Church were probably the most inadequate, but generally the dwellings in this area were of a good standard.

Stretching north-west from the roundabout and to the right of the present main road were two parallel rows, totalling fifty cottages, called Cyfarthfa Row. Built in 1840 the row facing the main road was later re-named Nantygweith Street. At the northern end of this row, near the entrance to the bus garage was the Nantygwenith Turnpike which was demolished in 1896. The houses of Cyfarthfa Row were four-roomed, double-fronted dwellings and when visited by the *Morning Chronicle* reporter in 1850 they were new. He was impressed not only by the quality of the accommodation offered, but also, in contrast to what he had seen only a matter of yards away, by the civilised nature of the inhabitants:—

"This was one of the roomiest and best cottages I had seen in the ironworks. It was new. It had a fine large kitchen, a good parlour, a convenient pantry with a window, and two lofty-ceilinged bedrooms up-stairs. There was a small strip of garden behind, and (mirabile dictu) a privy at command; there was one to every six houses in the row. Nevertheless the rent was only eight shillings a month. The house was literally crammed with furniture. In the kitchen were two mahogany chests of drawers, each of which supported a looking glass, a tea tray, a bread basket, tea caddies, and some books amongst which I observed Burhitt on the New Testament, folio, and Bagsters Comprehensive Bible. There was also a well polished eight day clock, and a set of mahogany chairs. On the wall were a quantity of prints in gold frames. Between two pieces of needlework was a portrait of Our Saviour upon one of the walls. Another had a good looking glass, a coloured portrait of the Duke of Wellington, and a large print of the Battle of Waterloo. From the rafters of the floor above hung a canary bird in his

50 Junction of George Street and Nantygwenith Lane. Some of the houses in Nantygwenith Lane were dwellings of only one room up and down. The wall of Cyfarthfa Church can be seen on the left

51 Williams Court, off Iron Lane

cage, a lanthorn, and a quantity of jugs enough to have supplied a harvest home supper. Over the fireplace there was displayed a bottle-jack, and small bellows, an Italian iron and flat-irons, extra tongs, poker and shovel, and a variety of useful little articles, all kept as bright as silver. The window was filled with a large myrtle. In the parlour was a good fourpost bedstead, a French-polished chest of drawers, covered with a profusion of glass and other articles, including a cruet stand and decanters, with small figures of the Queen and Prince Albert in china-ware, a neat work box, and some ornamental shells. In a corner was a glass-fronted cupboard, filled with china and glass, and ostentatiously displaying silver sugar tongs and a set of spoons. There was also a mahogany table with a bright copper tea-kettle reposing on it. On the walls were framed prints of St. John and St. Luke, with a portrait of King George the Fourth between them. Behind the door hung a quantity of male and female wearing apparel, and beside it were some shelves loaded with books. A slate, a hat, a bonnet and a pair of child's boots completed the inventory of this room. The apartments upstairs were equally well furnished. They had a four-post and a stump bedstead, mahogany chairs and tables, looking glasses, coffers for keeping clothes, a pair of scales for weighing flour, a spinning wheel and other conveniences. The floor-boards were as white as snow, and all the furniture was polished and kept with great care.''

The correspondent admits that this particular cottage was selected because it was the "first I met with where the furniture appeared remarkably good", but he goes on to describe other "average second-class" dwellings which, whilst not as extravagantly furnished as that described above, were nonetheless a complete contrast to what he had seen in Caedraw and Pontystorehouse areas.

Behind Cyfarthfa Row were the timber yards of the Cyfarthfa Works, the Glamorgan Canal and Chapel Row. This row of cottages and its immediate surroundings is one of the few areas of Merthyr where an attempt has been made at restoration and preservation. Four of the five houses of Chapel Row are still occupied while the fifth, the birthplace of Dr. Joseph Parry, is the headquarters of the town's Heritage Trust. It was in this cottage that the musician spent some of his boyhood years before the family's emigration to the ironmaking area near Danville, Pennsylvania in 1854. At the northern end of the row the outline of an octagonal building can be seen. Constructed originally as a chapel for workers in the Cyfarthfa Ironworks it later became a carpenter's shop and was remembered by some as the place where coffins and artificial limbs were manufactured.

Part of the canal has also been excavated at this point and a bridge which originally crossed the canal near Rhydycar Farm has been partially reconstructed. Adjacent to Chapel Row was the wagon shed, the one used in 1846 for the banquet which celebrated the wedding of Robert Thompson Crawshay to Rose Mary Yeates. Nearby, too, was a substantial graving dock where barges could be repaired and several hundred yards to the north the canal terminus itself. The close proximity of the canal to the Cyfarthfa Ironworks played an important part in its development, as iron could be loaded with minimum delay and the works benefitted considerably, generally at the expense of the three other iron making concerns.

Cyfarthfa Ironworks

The extent and layout of the Cyfarthfa Ironworks is best appreciated to begin with from a suitably elevated position, perhaps from Cyfarthfa Park or alternatively a point near to the Swansea Road. It is also best achieved with a map and some photographs to help with the interpretation, for what remains bears little resemblance to what Daniel Defore and George Borrow, who visited the works in the first half of the nineteenth century, saw as a wonder of the world. Between the construction of the first furnace by Anthony Bacon in 1765 and March 1875 when the old furnaces were finally extinguished, the works endured the vicissitudes of the nineteenth century iron trade, enjoying the years of boom but undergoing also the uncertainty and hardship associated with periods of slump. In the early part of the nineteenth century, it was reckoned to be the largest ironworks in the world. By the 1840's this accolade was attributed to Dowlais and by the early 1870's, through a combination of circumstances the Cyfarthfa Ironworks had declined to the point of almost total collapse.

Reconstruction as a steel making plant brought another quarter of a century of life for Cyfarthfa and relative prosperity for its workforce before the final blast furnace was stopped in 1910. Some of the plant was re-commissioned during the First World War but by then, even many of the buildings had become derelict.

Probably the earliest illustration of the Cyfarthfa Ironworks is Figure 52, an ink drawing made about 1806 by William Pamplin, a gardener employed by Richard Crawshay during his stay at Llwyncelyn House. Despite its primitive, almost child-like quality it is an excellent illustration of the organisation of the works at that time. On the hillside can be seen the heaps of raw materials in preparation, while on the left are the four blast-furnaces with covered charging houses and cast houses. The waterwheel in the centre is no doubt the giant constructed by Watkin George, Cyfarthfa's "mechanical genius". The building next to the waterwheel is the refinery where pig iron underwent a process preparatory to that of puddling, which made it malleable. This last process was carried out in the Old Forge on the right of the picture.

Figure 53, is an interior view of the Old Forge building, a water colour made by Penry Williams in about 1828. The lighted windows of the castle can be seen in faint outline in the top right-hand corner and the picture is full of life, clearly depicting the conditions in which the men toiled. To the

52 William Pamplin's drawing of the Cyfarthfa Ironworks. It shows four blast furnaces, the refinery and forge buildings with Watkin George's waterwheel in the centre

M.B.C.

53 Interior of the Old Forge at Cyfarthfa painted by Penry Williams   *M.B.C.*

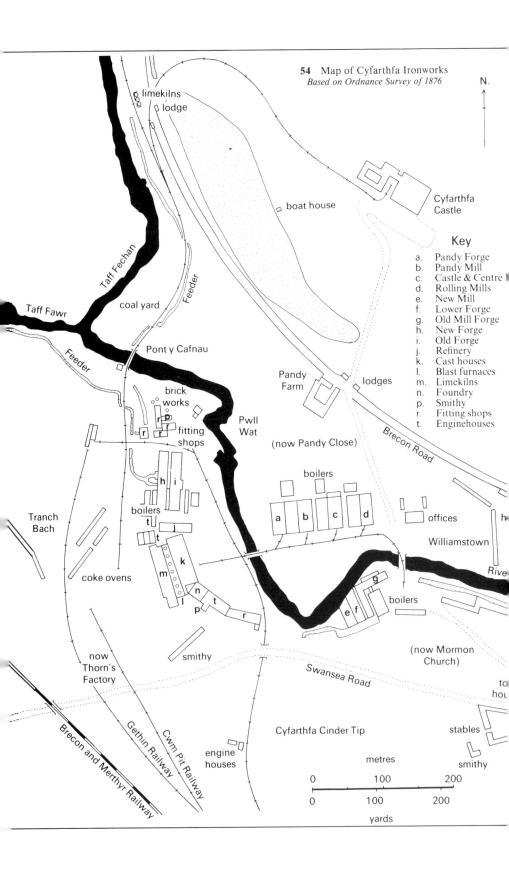

54 Map of Cyfarthfa Ironworks
Based on Ordnance Survey of 1876

N.

limekilns
lodge

boat house

Cyfarthfa
Castle

Key

a. Pandy Forge
b. Pandy Mill
c. Castle & Centre
d. Rolling Mills
e. New Mill
f. Lower Forge
g. Old Mill Forge
h. New Forge
i. Old Forge
j. Refinery
k. Cast houses
l. Blast furnaces
m. Limekilns
n. Foundry
p. Smithy
r. Fitting shops
t. Enginehouses

Taff Fechan

Feeder

Taff Fawr

coal yard

Pont y Cafnau

Feeder

brick
works

r p
r
fitting
shops

Pandy
Farm

lodges

Brecon Road

Pwll
Wat

(now Pandy Close)

boilers

h i

boilers
t
t j
t

a b c d

offices

h

Tranch
Bach

coke ovens

k
m

n
l p t
r

g

e f

boilers

Williamstown

River

(now Mormon
Church)

now
Thorn's
Factory

smithy

Swansea Road

to
hou

Cyfarthfa Cinder Tip

stables

Brecon and Merthyr Railway

Gethin Railway

Cwm Pit Railway

engine
houses

smithy

metres

0   100   200

0   100   200

yards

right are the puddling furnaces with the puddler working the iron with a long rod:—

"The puddler opened the aperture, that I might see the process, saying, "Look awhile into the furnace then shut your eyes, and on opening them you will see the iron". I did so. At first I could see nothing but a vapoury flame; however, on closing and suddenly opening my eyes, I saw the iron, white as snow, bubbling up with a hissing noise, like a simmering fluid. During this long process the puddler is either stirring with his lever the iron in the furnace or regulating the fire which he is enabled to do at convenience; consequently he is a bath of perspiration from the heat alone, not to speak of that which follows such heavy labour as he has to perform. These men look sallow and thin."

Immediately following the puddling the iron was shingled (i.e. either hammered or squeezed) to remove impurities and then rolled to produce bars about twelve feet long and three inches wide. These malleable bars might be re-heated to be rolled into rails in the rolling mills or for castings produced in the foundries.

The map, Figure 54, although surveyed in 1870 shows the works as it had been for some twenty years. By 1845 the seven blast furnaces were in production and there were few additions or alterations made to the general layout of the works after that date. The organisation was one of functional

55 Cyfarthfa Ironworks from the Castle terrace, about 1875

56 Base of one of the old Cyfarthfa blast furnaces showing the point where the pipe carrying the blast of air (tuyre) entered the furnace

simplicity with raw materials being received on the high ground above the furnaces. Here the coal was coked, impurities burnt from the ores in the calcining kilns and the limestone prepared before loading into the furnace. Each building played its part in successive processes, the finished rails being produced and made ready for despatch in the mills on the east bank of the river.

Although not of good quality, Figure 55, is worth study along with the map because it shows the works about 1860. Taken from almost the same viewpoint as Figure 52 in the foreground is the lake and behind, haystacks can be seen in the Pandy Farm. These would have been vital to feed the many horses employed in the works and associated collieries. In the centre of the photograph can be picked out the last remaining Cyfarthfa landmark, the high stone archway in the furnace retaining wall. Five blast furnaces can be counted to the right of the arch. Two others stood to the left of it. Ranged in front of the furnaces are the cast houses which were identical in design to those at Ynysfach (see Figures 44 and 45). The bases of these furnaces can still be visited, access being gained through the narrow archway at the northern end of the furnace bank. This is the entrance to the gallery which runs to the rear of the furnaces and from which each individual furnace is accessible. This gallery not only allowed access to the rear of the furnaces but also separated them from the hillside, thus preventing the percolation of water into the structure of the furnace which would have led to the rapid deterioration of the masonry. These furnaces have remained virtually untouched since the reconstruction of the works in the 1880's and are consequently in an extremely dangerous condition. The need to venture inside therefore is not imperative and Figure 56 shows the condition of the masonry almost twenty years ago. The tuyere pipe, which carried the blast of air into the furnace can also be seen.

The scene here was quite different in 1852 when our intrepid reporter from the *Morning Chronicle* visited the works:—

"The founder led me through an arched passage between two furnaces, so narrow as to admit only one at a time, into a chamber where the blast pipes divided and entered each furnace. It was utterly dark save at the points where the nozzle entered the furnaces. By stooping I was enabled to see the fluid iron or slag, or both trickling down like white threads, but the moment these came in the line of blast, they were dissipated and vanished. The noise was deafening; with the man's mouth to my ear it was impossible to make out what he said. I should add that we were followed by a man with a characteristic lantern—a long handled shovel covered with white-hot slag from the furnace; this however served to show the extent of the vaulted chamber in which we stood, and the form and diameter of the iron-bound hose of leather which conducted the blast to its destination".

Returning to Figure 55 for a moment, to the right of the furnaces can be seen two of the large and impressive Cyfarthfa blast-engine houses, while on the left, a third is also visible. These played an important part in generating power for the works and by 1850 there were five steam engines working here but waterpower was still at that time "the principal power employed at the Cyfarthfa works".

In his evidence to the Board of Health enquiry of 1849 Robert Crawshay said, "There are in all seven waterwheels; three of these are for driving rolling wheels, one for driving the lathes and grinding machinery, another for file grinding and roll turning. The other two wheels use water which formerly worked these above given. The largest wheels, three in number, are about fifty horsepower, and the smaller two about twenty-five horsepower''. The wheel which powered the machinery in the Old and New Forge buildings was thirty six feet in diameter and eight feet wide. It was notable in that it combined the features of an overshot, breast and undershot wheel, the water being capable of delivery at three different points.

Nothing remains at the site itself of the feeder network which supplied the waterwheels, the remnants disappearing about 1971. The feeder from the Taf Fechan still carries water to the lake in Cyfarthfa Park and the line of the Taf Fawr feeder, which took water from the river immediately below Cefn viaduct can still be seen. The lake in the park, of course, fulfilled more than an ornamental role, as it was important to the works for storing water during dry periods.

Figure 58 shows where the Taf Fechan and Taf Fawr feeders joined near the bridge which carried the tramroad from the Gurnos limestone quarries. The bridge, aptly named Pontycafnau, means the bridge of the troughs. The much published print from I. G. Wood's 'Rivers of Wales' of 1811 shows another bridge at this point, a somewhat elegant looking aqueduct which carried water across the river at a much higher level. The photograph also shows the line of the feeder on the opposite side of the river and

57   Pandy Farm and Pwll Wat with brick kilns

58 Pontycafnau (bridge of the troughs) at the junction of the Taff Fechan and Taff Fawr
feeders. The limekilns and one of the lodges can be seen in the distance

alongside that the tramroad to the quarries and the one which carried coal
up to the Castle for domestic purposes.

Pontycafnau (a cast iron bridge of unusual design but not unique and old
photographs indicate at least one other nearby) enables one to follow the
line of the old tramroad and feeder from the area of the works alongside the
Taf Fechan to the limekilns which can be seen in Figure 58 (also depicted on
the cover of this volume). There were once many limekilns in and around
the town, the product being an important commodity, used in the making
of mortar for building, whitewash for the cottages of the town, in tanning
and of course as an agricultural manure. The relatively modern concrete
building near the bridge housed a water driven turbine which provided
power for the town's electric trams, run by the Merthyr Traction Company.

From the limekilns, the tramroad first runs under the concrete bridge
which carries the present A.470 road, then under a much earlier stone
structure. It then continues between the river on one side and the lake feeder
on the other, to the site of the limestone quarries. Many stone sleepers can
be found along the route of the tramroad and the walk is a very pleasant one
through a nature reserve which is managed jointly by the Glamorgan
Naturalist's Trust and the Merthyr Borough Council. The quarry site is just
north of the Heads of the Valleys Road viaduct. In contrast to the narrow
valley one follows from Cyfarthfa, the valley floor here is wide and flat

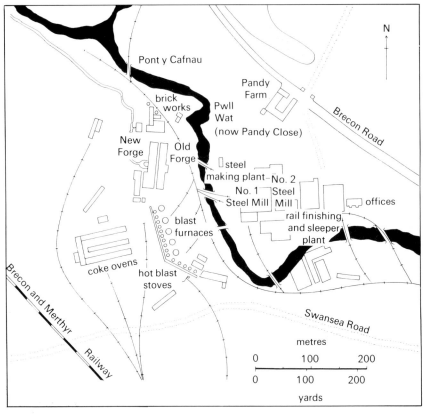

59 Map of Cyfarthfa Iron and Steel Works
Based on Ordnance Survey of 1900

where the limestone rock was removed. This area has recovered well from the ravages of the nineteenth century industry and is a very popular local recreation spot. Close investigation of the river bank will reveal the weir which diverts water into the Cyfarthfa feeder.

The reconstruction of the Cyfarthfa works as a steel works began in 1882 under the supervision of Mr. Edward Williams of Middlesborough. The tops of the old blast-furnaces were used as a platform on which the raw materials were deposited by an overhead gantry and from here the material was taken to the furnaces by two lifts. Five modern, iron-cased, closed top blast furnaces were built on the site of the old cast houses. Each of these furnaces was seventy feet in height and had an average make of 800 tons of iron per week. The blast which was supplied by six vertical direct-acting condensing blowing engines, was heated by the fifteen Cowper stoves ranged to the rear of the furnaces. Three of these blowing engines supplied by J. C. Stevenson of Preston, had steam cylinders of 33 inches and blast cylinders of 72 inches while the others, manufactured by Davy Brothers,

60 The Cyfartha Iron and Steel Works (about 1883) showing only four of the new blast furnaces complete   *M.B.C.*

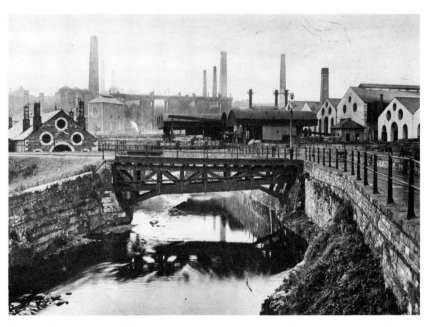

61 In this photograph all five blast furnaces have been built. Notice also the remodelling of the large enginehouse   *M.B.C.*

Sheffield had steam cylinders of 44 inches and 45 inches and 96 inch diameter air cylinders.

Figure 60 shows the works during the course of re-construction. Four furnaces have been completed, only the one on the far left remains to be built. The Cowper stoves and overhead gantry can also be seen and another point to note in comparison with Figure 61 is the enlarging and re-modelling of the enginehouse on the left of Figure 60. From the furnaces the slag was run into bogies which carried it to the tips while the molten iron was run into ladles which then transferred the metal to the Bessemer stages which were on the other side of the river. The four Bessemer converters each had a capacity of ten tons and adjacent to this plant were the rolling mills, the old Pandy and Castle mills being re-constructed as the No. 1 and 2 steel mills.

62 Running the molten iron from the furnace into the direct ladle to be conveyed to the Bessemer converter

63 Locomotive conveying the ingots and moulds to the ingot stripper. The ingots were removed from the moulds prior to re-heating

64 The new coke ovens

65 The derelict works   *M.B.C.*

The ingots were brought from the Bessemer shop on bogies drawn by three foot gauge locomotives, stripped of their moulds and charged into the soaking pit. These vertical furnaces reheated the steel ingots prior to rolling. The ingots were first cogged to blooms of about 7 inches square and then rolled to produce 120 feet of rail in 30, 40 or 60 feet lengths. In buildings nearby similar plant produced steel sleepers and other types of rolled steel.

Since the final closure of the works the site has seen many changes and a number of modern enterprises now occupy parts of the area. Thorn Lighting stands where once the coke ovens were; B.R.S. occupy the site of the Old and New Forges and at the base of the high wall Cyfarthfa Motors has taken over the area where the cast houses of the old works and the blast-furnaces of the steelworks once stood. On the opposite bank of the river the rolling mills site at first occupied by Rotax Ltd. during the Second World War and afterwards by Lines Brothers, makers of Tri-ang Toys, is now taken up by a number of smaller factories.

Glamorgan Canal

From the low output of the early years of their existence the production of Merthyr's ironworks expanded rapidly in the last two decades of the eighteenth century. This expansion relied in turn on the ability of the ironmasters to transport the iron from an area which was isolated and remote to Cardiff, from where it could be exported to the world's developing markets. The mountain-top road via Gelligaer and Caerphilly had been suitable only for panier laden mules, while the newly constructed turnpike following the river valley did little to come to terms with the needs of the industry in Merthyr.

The answer of course, was a canal, but the difficulties of such an undertaking proved to be varied and numerous. The distance to be covered was a mere twenty-four miles, but for most of its length the canal was confined to a narrow and heavily wooded valley. These problems were complicated further by the height difference between Merthyr and Cardiff, the drop of 540 feet necessitating the construction of forty-nine locks. The engineers employed were Thomas Dadford Senior and Junior and the canal was completed in 1794.

The importance of water as a means of producing power in the ironworks has already been mentioned, likewise the dearth of water for domestic purposes, particularly during dry summers. The needs of the canal created further difficulties as the concentration of locks on the nothern section between Abercynon (then called Navigation) and Merthyr was especially wasteful. At the southern end of the College car park, near the entrance to the modern pedestrian bridge stood lock number three, its attendant lock house and a small dock. The lock was better known as Parliament Lock and bears testimony to a dispute between Richard Hill of the Plymouth ironworks and the Glamorgan Canal Company over the right to extract water from the River Taff. This dispute, which originated as a result of Mr. Hill discovering the lock-keeper tampering with the supply of water to the Plymouth Works was eventually resolved through litigation and referred to the House of Lords. The present concrete weir replaced the old masonry structure at the time of the building of the new town centre in the late 1960's. From the site of Canal Square (occupying much of the car park) and the old wharf at Ynysfach, the course of the canal is easily followed between the waste tips of the Ynysfach Ironworks and the nearby collieries. Half a mile brings the walker to the Rhydycar Leisure Centre (an alternative car park for following these walks) and immediately to the west an area of derelict ground alongside the brook known as Nant Rhydycar (the lower part of Nant Cwmglo).

Rhydycar Cottages which stood on this area of waste ground were vacated following serious flooding from the stream in December 1979. Two elderly inhabitants died as a result of this calamity and the houses were left derelict. They were later demolished but six of the twenty-nine were removed to the Welsh Folk Museum at St. Fagans and are at present in the course of re-construction. The two rows, built almost at right-angles to each other, consisted of two room dwellings with an extra bedroom and larder at the back in an outshot which was covered by a catslide roof. This design of cottage belonged to a distinctive family of industrial house types associated with the Merthyr area, but more particularly with the Crawshay family and

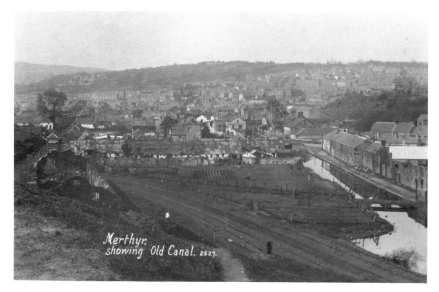

66 The Glamorgan Canal at Ynysfach. The remains of the refinery of the Ynysfach ironworks is on the left. The area in the foreground is now occupied by the Merthyr Technical College

67 Bridge at the entrance to Lock Number Two (near the present fire station)

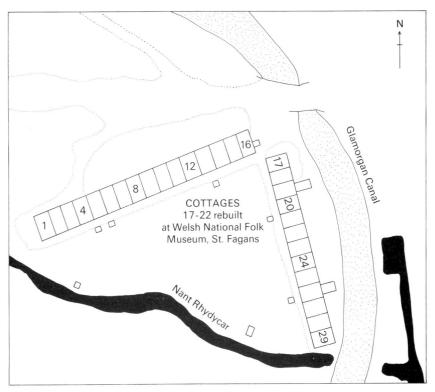

68 Plan of Rhydycar Cottages

69 Rhydycar Cottages before demolition, 1982

95

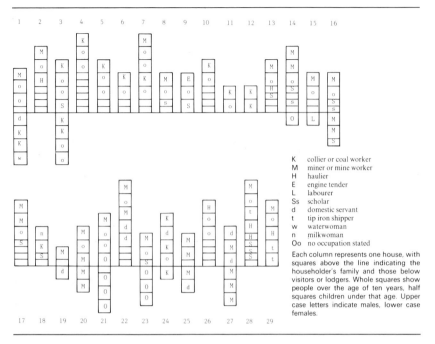

70 Rhydycar Cottages
Information based on the 1851 Census Returns

some two hundred and twenty of this pattern were built between 1795 and 1830. Similar houses were to be found at Ynysfach, Tranch Bach and Cyfarthfa Lane in Georgetown.

The cottages at Rhydycar were built to house coal and ironstone miners who worked in the levels and pits of the Cyfarthfa Iron Company. The 1851 Census shows some of the families to have originated in Carmarthenshire and Pembrokeshire although most were native to the town. An average of six persons lived in each of these cottages (two accommodated nine) and although conditions were far above other areas of Merthyr, little imagination is required to appreciate the difficulties endured by those who lived in these small houses.

Many of the males who lived here worked in the Rhydycar Pit which was only a few hundred yards away on the opposite side of the stream. There were two pits, a working and a pumping shaft. The outline of the garden belonging to a cottage which housed the pit farrier is still visible and the scant remains of a pumping enginehouse can also be seen. Although recorded as an ironstone mine on the 1875 Ordnance Survey Map, coal was also mined, the shaft being sunk 75 yards to the Gellideg Seam. Underground roadways linked this pit with Cwm Pit, Lower Colliers Row Pit and Ynysfach Drift. The engine at the top of the pumping shaft was a double acting Cornish Beam engine making ten strokes per minute.

96

71   Rhydycar Pumping Pit, 1967

Following the line of the Glamorgan Canal from Rhydycar will soon bring the walker to the point near Rhydycar Farm where the bridge, now in front of Chapel Row, used to cross the canal. It is at this point that one can decide to either continue south along the canal towards Abercanaid or follow the old parish road towards Graig Farm or Melin Canaid.

The former course takes one first past the abutments of the bridge which supported the Brecon and Merthyr Railway line on its long looping climb out of Merthyr station and towards Cefn Coed, and secondly under the skew arching of the bridge which carried the Vale of Neath line on its run down from the Aberdare Tunnel. The broad gauge Vale of Neath line, which was completed to the High Street terminus (present Merthyr Station) in 1853, was altered to mixed gauge in 1864.

The long incline from station to tunnel was the scene of a runaway one Saturday evening in May 1874 when twenty-one loaded wagons broke loose in the tunnel and ran back towards the station. A train waiting at Merthyr station was knocked with such force that it went straight through the buffer stops and the engine 'Antelope' was embedded in the wall. Fifty people were injured and one killed as a result of this mishap.

South of these bridges on a gentle curve in the canal stands Glyndyrys lock house and the site of the fourth and fifth locks below Cyfarthfa. Although the canal has been filled in for very many years it is still possible at this point to appreciate the height a barge would have been lifted as result of passing through the locks.

As a result of the difficulties the canal experienced with low water in times of drought, John Rennie the engineer was engaged to carry out a survey on

72 Cast iron bridge across canal near Rhydycar Farm, 1969. Now restored and re-erected near Chapel Row

73 Vale of Neath Railway and Brecon and Merthyr Railway bridges near Rhydycar Farm

74 & 75 Glyndyrys Lock House and grave of lock-keeper at Graig Chapel graveyard

the available water supplies and in consequence a large reservoir was constructed at Glyndyrys in 1806. This was situated behind the lock-house and the remains of the embankment and sluices can be found in the scrub woodland nearby. The lock was at one time kept by William Moses (Gwilym Tew o Lan Taf) a local bard, and also by Morgan Morgan whose grave in Graig Churchyard still proudly proclaims his occupation.

To the south of the lock-house is Upper Abercanaid, a small group of houses of both social and industrial interest. This community, built on the banks of the Canaid Brook once comprised some twenty houses, a pub, a Welsh Baptist chapel, several coal pits and a substantial canal dock. The Cyfarthfa mineral taking covered the whole of the west side of the Taff Valley from Nant Ffrwd in the north to Nant Canaid in the south, and Upper Abercanaid occupies, therefore, the extreme south-east corner of the take. At the northern end of Quay Row are the remains of Glyndyrys pumping pit. The engine at this shaft was well sited because the inclination of the coal bearing strata caused much of the water in the Cyfarthfa taking to drain to this point. The pit was 149 yards deep and sunk in 1839. At the head of the shaft was a Cornish double-acting pumping engine similar to that already noted at Rhydycar. The engine here, also worked a pump at Pwll Tasker sunk by George Tasker to the Nine Feet Seam at a depth of 50 yards. Tasker's Pit having been forgotten for many years, somewhat surprisingly came to light about fifteen years ago when it was re-discovered beneath a chicken cot.

The imposing house to the rear of Quay Row with its monkey puzzle (Chile Pine) tree, a hallmark of middle class gardens in nineteenth century Merthyr Tydfil, was the birthplace of Sir William Thomas Lewis, Baron Merthyr of Senghenydd. The boy, who was to begin work at thirteen apprenticed to his father (who was an engineer in the Plymouth Ironworks) was destined for great things. His engineering and entrepreneurial skills were to carry him to a pre-eminent position in the South Wales coal industry, becoming as he did, virtual overlord of the Lewis Merthyr Collieries, one of the most powerful coal combines in Britain. It is his statue which stands at the entrance to Merthyr General Hospital and it was he who was in part responsible for the erection of the Merthyr Fountain as a memorial to his antecedents, Robert and Lucy Thomas.

It was the Thomas family which is generally regarded as being responsible for bringing the attention of the outside world to the qualities of the Merthyr steam coal. Nearly all the coal mined locally was for consumption in the ironworks, but in 1828, a lease was taken out on the Waunwyllt property by Robert Thomas. Coal mined here supplied householders in Merthyr and Cardiff to begin with, but its qualities soon impressed men who were already trying to establish markets for steam coal mined in other parts of South Wales. Soon, the coal mined from the Four Feet Seam at Waunwyllt was much sought after and had established an exalted reputation among steam ship companies and navies alike.

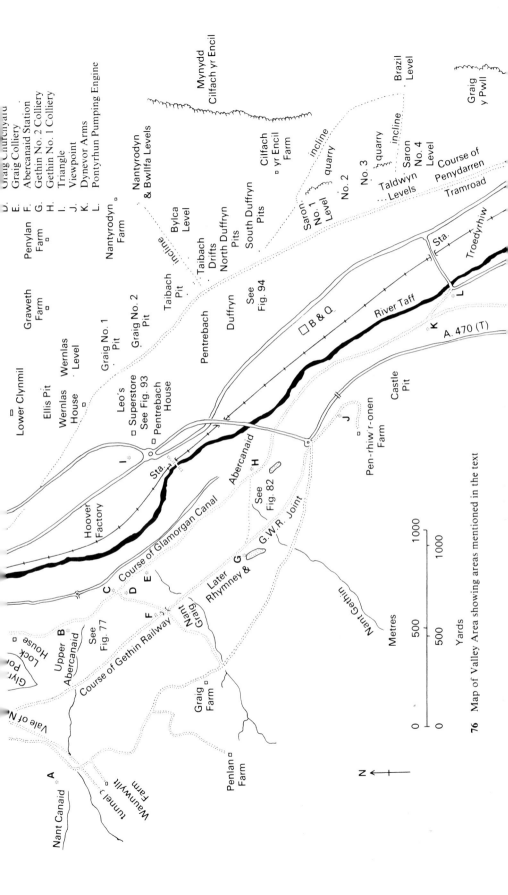

76 Map of Valley Area showing areas mentioned in the text

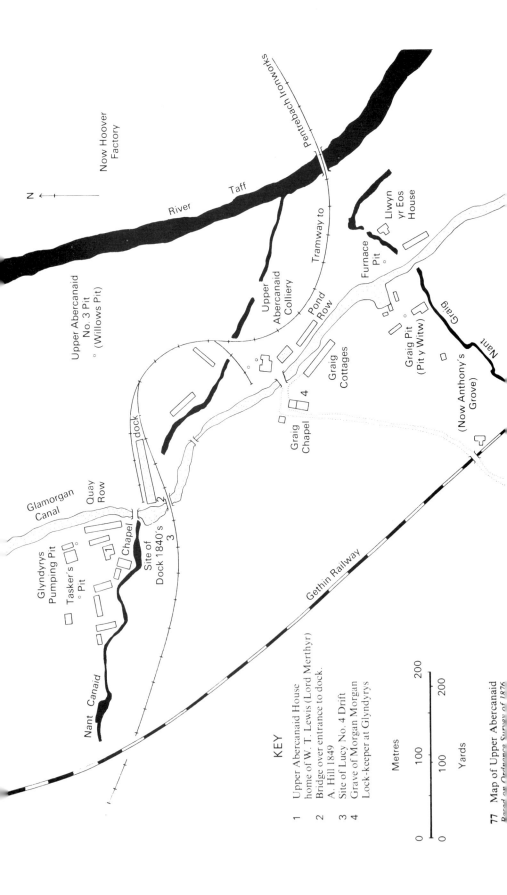

Now Hoover
Factory

N ←

River
Taff

Pentrebach Ironworks

Upper Abercanaid
No. 3 Pit
(Willows Pit)

Tramway to

Upper
Abercanaid
Colliery

Pond
Row

Furnace
Pit

Llwyn
yr Eos
House

Graig Pit
(Pit y Witw)

Nant Graig

(Now Anthony's
Grove)

Graig
Cottages

Graig
Chapel

4

dock

Glamorgan
Canal

Quay
Row

Chapel

Site of
Dock 1840's

2

3

Glyndyrys
Pumping Pit

Tasker's
Pit

1

Nant Canaid

Gethin Railway

KEY

1   Upper Abercanaid House
    home of W. T. Lewis (Lord Merthyr)
2   Bridge over entrance to dock.
    A. Hill 1849
3   Site of Lucy No. 4 Drift
4   Grave of Morgan Morgan
    Lock-keeper at Glyndyrys

Metres   100   200

Yards   100   200

0

77 Map of Upper Abercanaid
Based on Ordnance Survey of 1876

It is likely that some of these workings were established on the area of land directly opposite Abercanaid House. A level and old shaft are marked on the 1870 Ordnance Survey map and until relatively recently the remains of a shallow stone-lined shaft could be seen here. During the opening of the Lucy Number Four Drift by Thomas Merthyr Collieries in 1939 old workings in the Four Feet Seam were discovered very near to this point. There were also the remains of a small dock on the western side of the canal where coal could be loaded directly into barges. Following Robert's death in the mid 1830's the concern moved to the Graig property and established a mine only a few hundred yards south of the original workings.

On the other side of the canal at Upper Abercanaid there was a second and much larger dock. The remains of this were filled in during the building of the new 'Hoover' factory and the roundabout occupies the site. The dock was 260 feet long and 35 feet wide, and was entered under a towpath bridge. The bridge was of similar pattern to that re-sited at Chapel Row and marked A. Hill 1849. The dock was conveniently situated for the Plymouth Iron Company's works to import and export goods and raw materials.

Only a matter of yards from the dock, at the northern end of Pond Row, and opposite to where a track leaves the canal and leads towards Graig Farm, stood Upper Abercanaid Colliery. This was the only mine belonging to the Hill's Plymouth Company which took coal from the west of the River Taff. The cottages here take their name from the colliery pond, which was at their northern end.

78 Entrance to dock at Upper Abercanaid

79 Upper Abercanaid Colliery

A plan of this colliery drawn in 1847 shows that by that date quite extensive workings had already been established. The survey shows numbers one (pumping) and two shafts near the canal with Number 3 Pit (also called Willows Pit) some 250 yards to the north-east. Two adit entrances and three furnace shafts are also shown serving the workings in four different seams. This colliery was closed about 1860 because of an underground fire and not re-opened until 1883. By 1890, in order to maintain an output of approximately 5,000 tons of coal per week from five districts in the Six, Nine, Seven Feet and Gellideg Seams it was found necessary to install a new haulage system. Compressed air was considered for power but eventually electricity was found to be the more economical and practical. This underground electric haulage at Upper Abercanaid was to be one of the first of its type to work in a South Wales Colliery. It was of course the abandoned workings of this colliery which gave the engineers building the new Hoover Factory so many headaches. In order to provide secure foundations many thousands of tons of liquid concrete had to be poured into the cavities created by coal extraction a century before.

Opposite Pond Row was another row of cottages called Graig Cottages which would probably have accommodated the families of those working in Graig Pit or Pit y Witw (Widow's Pit) as it was called locally. This was the mine opened by Lucy Thomas following her move from Waunwyllt. The map (Figure 77) shows it to be ideally situated on the bank of the canal (immediately below the new houses called Anthony's Grove) with a convenient docking area where barges could be moored. Although never rivalling in terms of output the mines of the large iron companies (in 1861

104

Graig Chapel and Bridge.   Abercanaid.

80   Graig Chapel and Glamorgan Canal. This building was demolished because of
mining subsidence

for example the coal produced here was only one tenth of that produced at
Cyfarthfa), the mine played an important part in the history of the South
Wales coal industry. Because of a fear that an increase in production would
prematurely exhaust reserves, Lucy Thomas deliberately limited the output
and as a result turned away many prospective customers. One of these was
John Nixon, a Tynesider and sinker of pits in the Cynon Valley as well as
Merthyr Vale Colliery. The description of his visit to the pit in 1840 gives an
excellent picture of the scene here on the canal side:—

"On arriving at Graig Colliery, Mr. Nixon found himself in the midst of
the idyllic period of the coal trade. Mrs. Thomas—she may be called the
mother of the coal trade—was held to be carrying on a very good business.
She sat in her office, a wooden hut near the pit mouth, and traded for cash,
placing in a basket over her head the moneys which she received for her
coal. At the pit's mouth it may be said that the poetry of the Arcadian world
joined hands with the prose of a busier time to come. "Laughing girls", like
those who trod the wine press of old (save that they were grimy with coal
dust) handled the coal, sorting it by hand and picking out the lumps, which
were afterwards placed on boats, "as carefully as if each lump was an egg",
and Mrs. Thomas was then raising the amount, considerable in those days,
of 150 tons by the day.

"Mr. Nixon however, got no encouragement from Mrs. Thomas. Asked
if she would be prepared to produce more coal and supply some to him, the
old lady, perfectly contented with her business as it stood, made mention of
the "appalling" quantity of coal she was extracting from the bowels of the

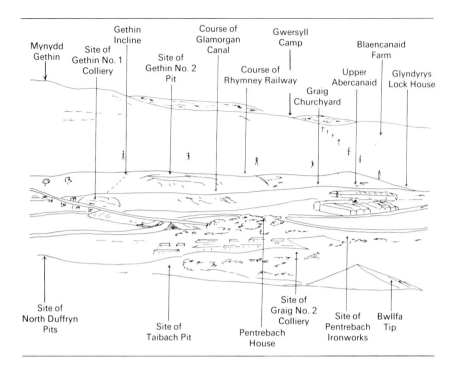

Gethin Incline
Mynydd Gethin
Site of Gethin No. 1 Colliery
Site of Gethin No. 2 Pit
Course of Glamorgan Canal
Gwersyll Camp
Course of Rhymney Railway
Blaencanaid Farm
Upper Abercanaid
Glyndyrys Lock House
Graig Churchyard

Site of North Duffryn Pits
Site of Taibach Pit
Site of Pentrebach House
Site of Graig No. 2 Colliery
Site of Pentrebach Ironworks
Bwllfa Tip

81 Panorama of Abercanaid Mountain and Taff Valley from Mynydd Cilfach yr Encil

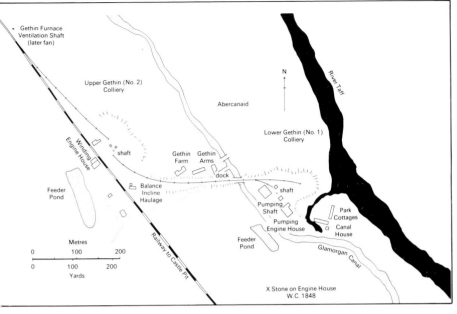

82 Map of Gethin Collieries at Abercanaid.
Based on Ordnance Survey of 1876

earth. Finally she informed Mr. Nixon that she would not undertake to produce more coal, or spare to him any coal at all''.

Prior to about 1845 the Cyfarthfa Iron Company produced sufficient coal to meet its own needs from the numerous levels and pits in the area to the north of the Canaid Brook. However, about that time Cyfarthfa's management began an investigation of the potential of an area of land west of the Taff but south of the Graig Estate. Two things probably motivated them in this. First was the anticipated exhaustion of existing coal reserves, for despite the large tract of land to the north of Nant Canaid, the seams had been worked for eighty years by extremely wasteful methods. The colliers simply drove a network of galleries leaving behind quite large pillars of coal. Frequently this method caused disturbances in floor and roof of the workings resulting in the crushing of the coal and the consequent abandonment of larges areas of coal seam. The second reason was the great interest being shown in the quality of the local steam coals, of which there were large untapped reserves south of Abercanaid. Up to this time only Hill's Plymouth had workings that far south and to secure the coal, deeper shafts would have to be sunk. To this end the Gethin Colliery at the southern extremity of Abercanaid was opened in 1849 and was to be one of Cyfarthfa's most extensive workings.

At the point where the canal finally leaves Abercanaid the walker passes Gethin Farm and Gethin House on the right. The farm is obviously of great age whilst the house was once the Gethin Arms, a public house which no doubt enabled the colliers who worked at Gethin to enjoy the opportunity to clear the dust of the pit from their throats. The site of Lower Gethin Pit (Gethin No. 1 Pit) is to the east of the canal's course immediately after one passes the abutments of an old bridge. The bridge was once part of the incline which linked Lower Gethin with Upper Gethin Pit (Gethin No. 2 pit) a few hundred yards up the hillside.

Four shafts were sunk to serve workings which were to extend over 180 acres, two working pits, a pumping and furnace shaft.

Lower Gethin was sunk only a matter of yards from the canal side. The working shaft, originally operated on the water balance principle, was 126 yards in depth (121 yards to the Four Feet Seam) and in common with many early pits in the area it was oval in shape. Alongside this shaft was a pumping pit only four yards deeper than its neighbour. The Upper Gethin pit can be visited by following the road which passes through Gethin Farm and leads to the top of the incline which linked the two pits. A concrete capped shaft and some stonework can be found, some of the latter belonging to the building which housed the haulage engine at the top of the incline. This pit was sunk 188 yards to the Nine Feet Seam. Remains of the

83   Lower Gethin colliery showing pumping enginehouse and fan buildings

84 Haulage enginehouse at top of the Gethin Incline with the winding enginehouse
of Gethin Number Two Colliery in background

furnace shaft can be found about 400 yards north of the pit near to the point where the colliery sidings met the main railway. This line was originally called the Gethin Railway and linked the colliery with the Cyfarthfa works. It was extended in the 1860's to Castle Pit at Troedyrhiw and was later taken over as part of the Rhymney/G.W.R. Joint Railway up the western side of the Taff Valley.

The fact that the Cyfarthfa Company continued to use water balance at Gethin No. 1 is somewhat surprising as the system worked best where there was free drainage from the workings, as in their mountainside pits between Heolgerrig and Upper Abercanaid. There was no free drainage at Gethin and any water taken into the pit as a result of using the water balance system had to be pumped back out. By 1870 however, Gethin No. 2 Pit does seem to have had a steam winding engine, as the O.S. Map of that date indicates the existence of an enginehouse. The other point of interest as far as the organisation of the colliery is concerned is the utilisation of furnace ventilation. This system (already mentioned in conjunction with Upper Abercanaid Colliery) was widely used throughout the British coalfields and relied on the current of air created when a furnace was positioned near the bottom of a shaft. The hot air rising in that shaft (called the upcast) caused fresh air to be drawn down another (the downcast) and circulated around the workings of the colliery. This was an inefficient and dangerous means of ventilation. It was to have dire consequences for this colliery, being responsible for two explosions which occurred in 1862 and 1865.

The first explosion occurred on 19th. February 1862 killing forty-seven men and boys. Many of these were from the Georgetown area and left twenty-three widows and fifty-seven fatherless children. At the inquest which followed, a verdict of manslaughter was brought against John Moody the 'Viewer' of the colliery. The ventilation of the pit was found to be deficient in quantity, badly arranged and liable to frequent interruption. It was also agreed that the use of naked lights had played an important part as the source of the ignition. Sad to say by 1865 little had changed and another thirty-four men died as a consequence:—

Cardiff & Merthyr Guardian, Wednesday, December 20th.,

"About 9 o'clock a messenger arrived at Cyfarthfa announcing a dreadful explosion at Gethin Colliery.

The explosion occurred at five minutes past eight and was immediately made known to persons working at the pit and those at the shaft mouth.

It occurred in the eastern workings of the Nine Feet Seam and in a spot where a danger signal indicating the presence of 'fire' had been placed a day or so previously.

The explosion was not as violent as former ones, six men being burnt to death but fully twenty-six or twenty-eight suffocated.

On proceeding to the scene immediately after the occurrence we found the old picture. First the great cover over the pit's mouth, then a dense crowd of people and in the midst close by the shaft a heap of straw for the dead bodies and near them the medical gentlemen and agents of the works. As each body was brought up it was taken to the heap of straw and every possible means used to restore life. The signal for lowering the carriage is made by striking a metal bar and this sound came sharply, fiercely and towards the end angrily.

We have never seen a spectacle—such a scene of horror. Those burnt were so charred about the face that any feature might have been broken off as one breaks a piece of charcoal. Their hair was burnt away; hands clotted like jelly''.

In the explosion, John Luke and Vavasour Rees died with their sons David (11 years) and William (15 years). Five others of those who died were under sixteen years of age whilst one, Rees Davies was seventy-five years old. The death of John Rees aged sixteen from the Brecon Road would no doubt have considerable effect on his family of mother, seven brothers and two sisters as his father had been killed three years earlier in Roblin's Pit, Cyfarthfa.

In evidence given to the inquest held on those who died, Selah Thomas, a Gethin collier told of his experiences on the morning of the explosion:—

"On Wednesday morning he descended the pit with many others and saw Thomas, one of those killed, in the lamproom as they were getting their lamps ready. He worked in the same vein as Thomas but further away.

Thomas remarked to them that his old stall, a disused one called No. 11 was full of gas, so was his brother Tom's. The gas was so abundant that it came out of the stall into the partings, a place where there was considerable thoroughfare. They, however, went into work but in about an hour he felt a ringing noise in his ears. He started up and a companion shouted that the "damp is off", meaning that there had been an explosion.

He rushed away and met a man who ran too, in the same direction; but suddenly the man stopped and retracing his steps into the gloom of death they had left, said "I must go back for the boy" and went back and fell among the dead".

As in 1862 the findings of the inquiry pointed the accusing finger at the colliery management for failing to ensure the safe running of the mine.

The route south from Gethin Colliery will take you under the viaduct of the new A.470(T) road and towards Troedyrhiw. Sadly, construction of the new road has obliterated remains of another Cyfarthfa pit, the Castle Colliery which was the very last to be sunk by the company in 1869. It was also its deepest, reaching the Gellideg Seam at 388 yards.

If there could have been any fitting monument to coal mining in the Merthyr area, it would have been the winding enginehouse at Castle Pit. Constructed in 1863, in the Cyfarthfa tradition, with dressed limestone decoration of quoins, windows and doors, it stood in glorious contrast to those drab affairs of the Plymouth Company across the valley at Duffryn. To me it represented the final fling of the Crawshays, whose enginehouses

85   Castle Colliery at Troedyrhiw (about 1875)

86   Winding enginehouse at the Castle Pit (1965)

looked as if they were built to last for ever. Later buildings at the site, the haulage enginehouse built in 1899 for example, were shoddy in comparison. Rough grey pennant had replaced the limestone and brick had been substituted for those magnificent limestone blocks.

Castle Pit was not however Cyfarthfa's first venture this far south, as they had worked the Castell Wiever Seam (No. 2 Rhondda) from a shallow shaft known as Daniel Jenkins' Pit from quite a number of years beforehand. The concrete capped shaft of this small colliery can still be located on the northern edge of the council estate near the Dynevor Arms. This pub must now be one of only a few remaining of the many which were once to be found along the banks of the canal, serving the needs of those who either worked on the canal itself or in nearby pits and ironworks.

From the Dynevor one can descend along Ash Road to the river at Pontyrhun (Rhun's Bridge). The bridge reputedly stands near the place where Rhun, son of Brychan, was killed whilst trying to defend his sister Tudful and other members of his family, who were being pursued by a band of murderous Picts.

More recently, the western end of the bridge was the site of a massive enginehouse which pumped water from the River Taff into the canal. Built as a consequence of Rennie's survey of 1806 it was strategically sited at a point where water used in the Plymouth, Pentrebach and Duffryn ironworks was returned to the river. The enginehouse was erected by Mr. J.

87 Ash Road with Castle Colliery in background *Geraint James*

88 Bridge Street Troedyrhiw and pumping enginehouse for the Glamorgan Canal
Geraint James

Griffiths, an engineer in the Cyfarthfa Ironworks, and housed an engine which lifted eight to ten tons of water per minute the eighty feet from the river to the canal. On its demolition much of the stone from this building went to construct the church at Merthyr Vale.

Hendre Fawr and Cwm Pit

From Rhydycar Farm the old parish road will take you first across the course of the Brecon and Merthyr Railway, over the Ynysfach Railway and under the Gethin Railway to a point on the old Cwm Pit Line near the site of Lower Colliers Row. Although close to the town's centre, it is quiet, with some secluded pieces of woodland where in spring redstart and pied fly-catcher nest with more common species, and old balance ponds provide interesting habitats for a wide variety of flowers and insects. Generally one can wander at will here, or perhaps try to follow the many old tramways or inclines which linked the levels and pits with the major arterial lines running towards the Cyfarthfa Works. Quiet now maybe, but once alive with industry as the many tips and depressions caused by mining testify.

Close at hand are the heaps of rubble from the demolition of Lower Colliers Row cottages and near to this point, too, it is possible to find part of the course of the old Cyfarthfa Canal. C. Hadfield, in his book on canals of South Wales, says that it was probably cut in the late 1770's by Anthony Bacon and carried tub-like boats approximately 14 feet long by 8 feet wide. The waterway, a canal only in the most primitive sense of the word, started near the Canaid Brook, followed the contours of the hillside and passed near the mouths of many levels to effect a cheap and relatively efficient means of transporting ore and coal to Cyfarthfa. An embankment which once formed part of the canal can be found beyond the tips in the woodland towards Cwm Pit. The course, followed towards the Canaid Brook, termin-ates in a quite large feeder pond which at one time played an important part in the working of the canal.

If one takes the old track leading up onto the mountainside, some panoramas of the town and valley are offered from the tops of the well grassed tips on the left. These tips were formed of coal waste from the Cwm Pit and Cwmfelin Drift.

Several hundred yards along the track, a tributary of the Canaid crosses it, and if one is prepared to brave the dense conifer plantation, following the stream for about 500 yards will bring one to the remains of a small iron furnace. Little is known of this sixteenth century Blaencanaid furnace which underwent excavations in 1965. It is sited near a small waterfall on the brook which would have provided power for a bellows. A small charging platform was uncovered above the furnace itself which would have been no more than twelve feet in height. In front of the furnace the casting floor was revealed and also walls of a building which would have given those who worked the furnace some protection from the elements. After clearing the vegetation and some overlying soil in 1965 it was possible to make some sense of the site's layout, but unfortunately a further twenty years of plant growth has left much of what was revealed then, quite indistinguishable.

Returning to the track, a hundred or so yards will bring you to Melin Canaid the site of one of the area's once numerous corn mills. Like the furnace, the mill was well sited to take advantage of the driving power of a nearby stream. Dating from before 1715 the mill would have played an important part in the agricultural economy of this area in pre-industrial times.

Past Melin Canaid the track climbs more steeply towards Hendre Fawr Farm. The name (Hen—old, Dre—settlement, fawr—large) suggests a sizeable settlement of some antiquity, but the ruins do little to support this assumption. The initials R.I. and the date 1796 chiselled into a coarse sandstone block beneath one of the large sycamores alongside the ruins give only a hint of the homestead's history. The 1851 Census shows that the Williams family farmed here, supported by no less than six farm labourers and a housemaid. One cannot help wondering however, whether the name refers to a much earlier period in the area's history, for a short distance away, on the ridge between Cynon and Taff, but surrounded now by the pernicious conifer, are the iron age settlements of Gwersyll and Buarth Maen.

89   Derelict buildings at Cwm Pit in the 1930's

115

90 Collier officials, Cwm Pit.
David Jones (Dai Gelli) on the left was a contractor at Cwm Pit at the turn of the century   *Eira Smith*

For the time being, until the sitka spruce planted below take it away, Hendre Fawr offers grand views of the valley below and the opportunity perhaps to ponder the changes which might have been observed from this spot since the anonymous mason made his mark.

Looking towards Penylan Hill from Hendre Fawr the site of the ventilation shaft for the Vale of Neath Tunnel and a small quarry where sandstone blocks were quarried for use in the lining of the tunnel can be seen. To reach these involves some quite arduous walking as the ridges and furrows created by the Forestry Commission have to be crossed. From the area of the quarry however, things do become easier as a well made track leads down to Waunwyllt Farm and onto the parish road.

Alternatively, one may return from Hendre Fawr towards Melin Canaid, leaving the track at a point where it is crossed by an old watercourse. If followed, this will take you to the pond which belonged to Cwm Pit. This small reservoir would have been the balance pond for the pit when it was

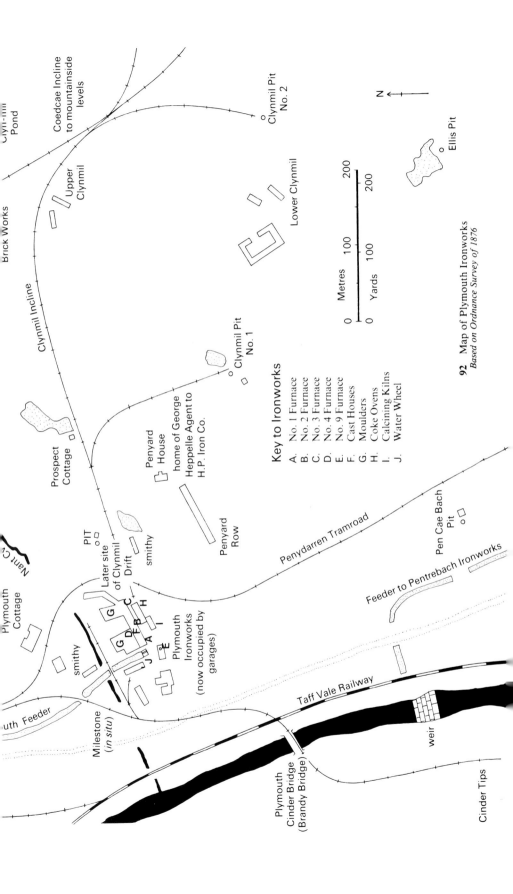

Clynmil Pond

Coedcae Incline to mountainside levels

Upper Clynmil

Brick Works

Clynmil Incline

Clynmil Pit No. 2

N

Ellis Pit

Lower Clynmil

Prospect Cottage

Penyard House

home of George Heppelle Agent to H.P. Iron Co.

Clynmil Pit No. 1

Metres		100		200
0		100		200
Yards				

0

92 Map of Plymouth Ironworks
Based on Ordnance Survey of 1876

Nant C...

PIT

Later site of Clynmil Drift

smithy

Penyard Row

Key to Ironworks

A. No. 1 Furnace
B. No. 2 Furnace
C. No. 3 Furnace
D. No. 4 Furnace
E. No. 9 Furnace
F. Cast Houses
G. Moulders
H. Coke Ovens
I. Calcining Kilns
J. Water Wheel

Plymouth Cottage

smithy

G G D F B C H
J A I
E

Plymouth Ironworks (now occupied by garages)

Penydarren Tramroad

Pen Cae Bach Pit

Feeder to Pentrebach Ironworks

...uth Feeder

Milestone (*in situ*)

Taff Vale Railway

Plymouth Cinder Bridge (Brandy Bridge)

weir

Cinder Tips

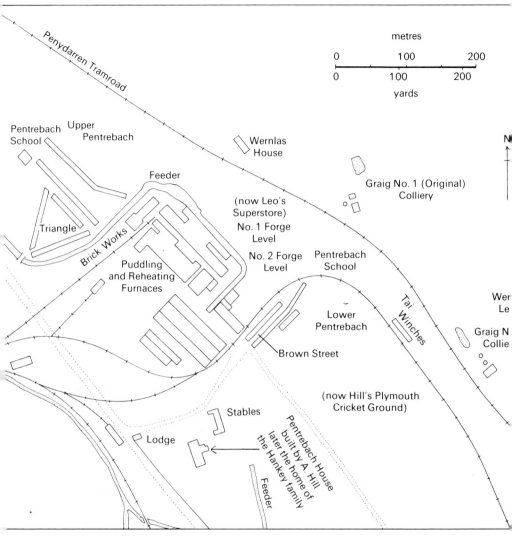

93 Map of Pentrebach Ironworks
Based on Ordnance Survey of 1876

spectacular panoramas, local people have found it difficult to relate the new route to what had become so familiar on the course of the old road and there are several places where one feels it would be enjoyable to pull off, stop and study the view at one's leisure.

At the northern end of the new section, before it descends towards Pentrebach, a minor road leaves the roundabout and climbs towards Penrhiw'r onen Farm. On this road, near to the site of the old Castle Colliery, there is ample opportunity to view a large area of the upper Taff Valley, with the peaks of the Brecon Beacons in the distance. More particularly it is an ideal spot to view the area of the valley which was worked by the Hill's Plymouth Iron Company, stretching between the small valley of Cwm Blacks and the village of Troedyrhiw. The older streets of this valley settlement were built to accommodate skilled Plymouth ironworkers with later dwellings housing those who worked at South Duffryn, Castle and Merthyr Vale Collieries.

If a visit to the site of the Cyfarthfa Ironworks is somewhat disappointing, a similar excursion to the three sites which constituted the Plymouth Ironworks can be reckoned as positively depressing. Each of the three ironworks and numerous pit sites has, during the last twenty years, succumbed to the attentions of land reclamation schemes. This leaves a swathe of featureless and uninteresting land which defies the imagination and curbs the enthusiasm of the most ardent industrial archaeologist.

The most notable remains are those of a tunnel which was part of the Penydarren Tramroad and ran to the rear of the blast furnaces at the Plymouth Works. This is to be part of a scheme of preservation initiated by the Merthyr Heritage Trust, but apart from this the remains most in evidence are stretches of feeder which carried water to drive machinery in the works.

From our viewpoint all three sites can be seen; the Plymouth site is to the north-east at a point now occupied by Baker's Garage; the Pentrebach site on derelict land adjacent to the roundabout and the site of Leo's Store; the Duffryn site is directly opposite, across the road from the B. & Q. Store.

The original site was developed on land leased from the Earl of Plymouth by John Guest and Issac Wilkinson. Anthony Bacon was also to have a financial interest in the concern, but by 1786 it was leased to Richard Hill. When he took over the works it consisted only of one small furnace, two giant bellows twenty-five feet high worked by one large waterwheel. After acquiring additional capital and two partners in 1803, Hill was able to expand the enterprise, a third furnace being built in 1807 and a fourth in 1815. It was about this time too that the development of the Pentrebach and Duffryn works began. Puddling and rolling mills were constructed at Pentrebach and in 1819 the first furnace was erected at Duffryn. Furnaces six and seven were put into blast at Duffryn in 1824 and a new rolling mill built at Pentrebach in 1841. In 1834 the seven blast furnaces of the company were capable of making 500 tons of pig-iron weekly. The blast for the Plymouth furnaces was supplied by two waterwheels, each eight feet wide and having a head of twenty-eight feet, whilst those at Duffryn were fourteen feet wide. Unlike the Dowlais works which installed its first steam engine in 1793, the Plymouth Company shunned the use of steam until the 1830's when the newly installed engine had a steam cylinder of 52½", a blowing cylinder of 123" and a stroke of eight feet.

The works were put up for sale in 1834 but no buyer could be found. As a result it continued in the ownership of the Hill family until Anthony's death in 1862 when it was purchased by Messrs Hankey, Fothergill and Bateman.

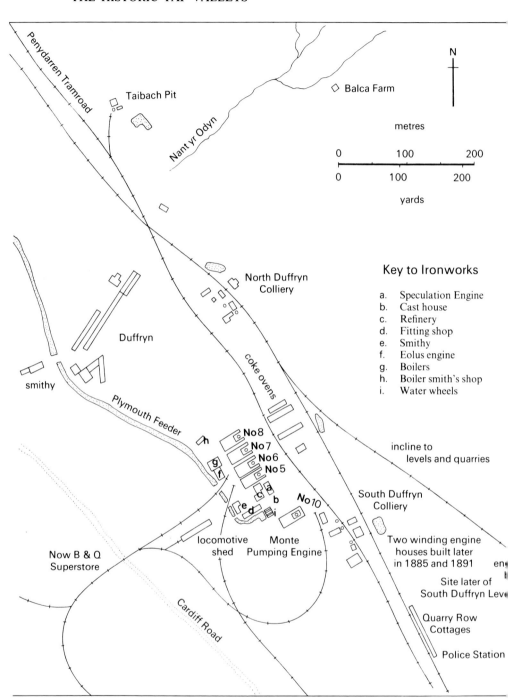

Key to Ironworks

a. Speculation Engine
b. Cast house
c. Refinery
d. Fitting shop
e. Smithy
f. Eolus engine
g. Boilers
h. Boiler smith's shop
i. Water wheels

94 Map of Duffryn Ironworks and collieries
Based on Ordnance Survey of 1876

The works continued to decline, ceasing to manufacture iron by 1880 and was once again offered for sale in 1882 when the property comprised:—

"2,400 acres, with a large extent of superior steam coal, well known as Hill's Plymouth and Merthyr Smokeless Coal. The whole of the unworked coal is estimated as 46,049,400 tons.

Plymouth Furnaces, five in number, the Pentrebach puddling furnaces and the Duffryn Blast Furnaces, five in number, are of great extent and readily adaptable for steel production.

Thomas's Take a very important property comprising 511 acres. The Original Pit, with pumping engines and the necessary appliances and boilers capable of working 200 tons daily. South Pit working 500 tons daily and Graig Pit with one pumping and winding engine, boiler and sheds.

Pentrebach Forges and Mills. These works consist of extensive sheds covering all the rolling mills and appliances, offices, fitting shops, carpenters shops, locomotive sheds, smith's shop and brick works.

North Duffryn Pits. One used as pumping and one used formerly as upcast, one pair of winding engines, one pumping engine with necessary boilers and sheds. Working three months in the year.

South Duffryn Pits. One pumping pit, Monte. One winding pit, Velocity. One upcast No. 1 south; engine sheds and smith's shops, boiler sheds. One old level on the mountain—stopped.

Abercanaid. Three pits, Nos. 1, 2 & 3 all stopped. Engine houses, sheds and appliances, these are situated near canal wharfage which is connected to the works.

Duffryn Ironworks. These works consist of five blast furnaces and appliances, forty-two coke ovens, engine houses, carpenters' shops, furnace manager's office.

Pentrebach House is a superior residence with lodge, offices, coach house, stabling and extensive out buildings, pleasure grounds, gardens and land. Four other residences or agents houses, two adjoining Pentrebach House, farm bailiff's house at Duffryn and one hundred and ninety-six cottages".

From 1882, under the control of the Hankey Family, the development of the large reserves of good quality steam coal was given priority. The management of the works was entrusted to Mr. Thomas Henry Bailey of the Birmingham firm of S. J. Bailey, Civil Engineers, and the enterprise took on the new title of Hill's Plymouth Company Ltd. Large tracts of coal were mined in the Six, Nine, Seven and Lower Four Feet seams from Graig and South Duffryn Collieries, as well as the modernisation and development of Upper Abercanaid Colliery. Many of the company's other pits (some mining ironstone originally) were abandoned or were kept as pumping or ventilation shafts.

Although there was a concentration on the shaft mining of its highly acclaimed steam coals, the company continued to mine bituminous coals

95 The Triangle, 1975

Ancient Monuments Commission

from levels driven into the valley sides. Some, like the four Saron Levels which had been producing coal since the 1850's, were ventilated by furnaces and had quite extensive workings, albeit only in one seam. The abandonment plan for these levels, dated February 1913, gives the name of the seam mined as alternatively, Kilfach yr Incil Vein, Saron or No. 3 Rhondda Seam. The plan shows the major roadways running east and north-east some 1500-2000 yards to the company's boundary and others almost a mile in the direction of Penddeucae Farms. The area of coal mined south of the No. 4 Level was what would have been termed dip workings, into which water would have naturally drained. As a consequence, working conditions were very wet although by 1900 electric pumps had been installed in an attempt to improve matters. This particular seam, having a fireclay floor and rock roof was thin, only 2′ 8″ in section with only 2′ 4″ of good coal.

Below are listed, along with the seams they worked, the drifts and levels worked by the Hill's Plymouth Company in the first three decades of this century.

		Date of Abandonment
Numbers 1, 2, 3 and 4 Saron Levels	No. 2 Rhondda Seam	1913
Nantyrodyn and Bwllfa Levels	No. 2 Rhondda Seam	1937
Gilfach Level	Gilfach Seam	1935
Numbers 1, 2 and 3 Taldwyn Levels	Taldwyn Seam	1935
Penlan Level	Hafod Seam	1935
Bylca Level	Hafod Seam	1935
South Duffryn Level (Boat Level)	Hafod Seam	1935
Wernlas Level	Upper 2′ 9″, Upper Four Feet seams	1935
Numbers 1 and 2 Forge Levels	Red Coal	—
Clynmil Drift	Lower 2′ 9″, 5′ 6″ and Lower Four Feet Seams	1902

The dates given above indicate when abandonment plans were submitted, but in a number of cases there is evidence to suggest that some workings were re-opened, Clynmil Drift for instance produced large amounts of coal during the First World War. Most evidence of these workings had disappeared along with that of pits and ironworks, only a few tell-tale depressions and the occasional spoil heap hinting at their one-time existence. Two quite prominent examples are those of the Brazil Level, high on the mountainside on the line of the Brithdir Seam but abandoned since 1897, and the Bwllfa/Nantyrodyn Levels. The spoil heap, adjacent to the latter is rather misleading, as it gives the impression that very large quantities of coal might have been removed from the mountainside. The truth is however, that the incline which still climbs the hillside, as well as carrying coal from the levels also carried spoil to be tipped from South Duffryn Pits. Up until the end of 1985 the site of these levels was well worth a visit as some haulage machinery remained *in situ*, and the three entrances (Bwllfa Level, Nantyrodyn Level and the fan ventilation drift) remained open. This however, is not now the case, as the site has been bulldozed in an attempt to seal the entrances and make them safe.

It might perhaps be of value at this point to mention the confusion which can arise when making a study of the seams mined by the various pits and levels in the Merthyr Area. The difficulty usually stems from the fact that the companies which mined the coal adopted different names for the various seams. This sometimes resulted from a desire to utilise what might have been a local name for the seam (e.g. Kilfach yr Incil Vein, a corruption of Cilfach yr Encil; Saron Seam, perhaps from the levels close proximity to Saron Chapel); sometimes it arose from a genuine confusion as to what seam was actually being worked, for it must be realised many of the seams in the Merthyr area were worked from the beginning of the nineteenth century when surveying techniques were primitive and the science of geology in its infancy; on occasions there might have been a deliberate attempt to confuse prospective customers as to the quality of the coal. The following list contains only a selection of the different names used by the coal companies to identify the seams they mined.

Brithdir Seam	Little Vein (Perthygleision Colliery, Aberfan)
No. 2 Rhondda Seam	Castell Weiver Seam (Daniel Jenkins' Pit, Troedyrhiw) Saron Seam Kilfach yr Incil Vein } Saron Level, Rhondda No. 3 Seam } Hill's Plymouth
Two Feet Nine Seam	Yard Little Six } Cyfarthfa Upper 2′ 9″ Upper Clynmil Hill's Plymouth Little Graig, Abercanaid
Six Feet Seam	In some collieries this seam was mined as two separate seams, e.g. South Duffryn Colliery as the Top Six Feet and Bottom Six Feet. At Dowlais it was called the Big Coal.
Nine Feet Seam	This too occurred as two separate seams at South Duffryn, the top coal was known as the Red Coal, the bottom was called the Nine Feet. At Dowlais the seam was called the Rhas Las.
Seven Feet Seam	Five Feet Six Inches Hill's Plymouth.
Five Feet/Gellideg Seams	These coal seams at South Duffryn occurred as three separate seams and were called the Top, Middle and Bottom coals of the Lower Four Feet Seam.

In 1893 the Hill's Plymouth Collieries employed 2,500 men and produced 403,833 tons of coal. By 1911 output had increased to 567,895 tons and large tonnages continued to be produced up until 1920. The following table for 1917 illustrates the relative importance of individual pits and levels whilst the second for 1930 indicates the decline of the concern as well as giving numbers employed at each workplace.

Large and Small Coal raised 1917

	Large	*Small*
No. 1 South Pit	93,866	51,256
No. 2 South Pit	37,363	19,081
South Duffryn Level	33,206	23,193
Graig Pit	64,529	27,081
Forge Levels	7,192	nil
Taibach Pit	12,725	11,241
Abergorki Level	2,153	1,267
Wernlas Level	15,504	6,944
Nantyrodyn Level	6,158	7,008
Clynmil Level	42,693	18,663

1930	*Nos. Employed*	*Coal Output*
No. 1 South Pit	203	48,834
No. 2 South Pit	433	116,400
Graig Pit	598	167,456
South Duffryn Level	121	33,250
Taldwyn Levels	56	24,436
Wernlas Level	70	21,294
Bwllfa/Nantyrodyn Levels	109	25,890

In the 1930's Castle Pit and South Duffryn Pits, having been acquired by Powell Duffryn Associated Collieries, were linked by an underground roadway and all coal was raised at South Duffryn. By the beginning of the Second World War however, all coal production had come to an end.

Following Nationalisation the winding enginehouses at South Duffryn accommodated electrical plant for submersible pumps which continued to drain the workings as it was thought the flooding of the mine might jeopardize Merthyr Vale Colliery. Pumping continued for almost thirty years after the colliery closed and up until the mid-1960's there were many interesting remains to be seen. The No. 5 Blast Furnace, speculation enginehouse, cast house, refinery and wheel pit of the Duffryn Iron Works all survived as did the two winding enginehouses, the Monte pumping enginehouse and other buildings associated with South Duffryn Colliery. After the Aberfan Disaster the remains of the ironworks were covered by pit waste from Merthyr Vale Colliery and other buildings were demolished. By 1975 two land reclamation schemes, one at Cwm Blacks and other at Pentrebach and Duffryn effectively eradicated all other remains. The massive tips which had been piled to the east of the old A.470(T) road were used to raise the level of the fields to the west (now occupied by B & Q Superstore and small factories).

96 Nantyrodyn and Bwllfa Levels

97 Remains of balance haulage in quarry

98 Taldwyn Levels

99 South Duffryn Level (Boat Level)

The car park at B & Q is a convenient starting point for walking the area of mountainside below Mynydd Cilfach yr Encil, and the old incline provides a reasonably easy means of climbing to a viewpoint high on the valley side.

If one chooses to climb to the crest of the ridge at almost 1,500 feet the views to the north across Merthyr Common towards Twyn-y-Waun, Dowlais and the Beacons beyond are indeed spectacular and well worth the effort. This elevated viewpoint offers a different perspective of the valley to that enjoyed from the mountainside around Cwm Glo, and on a clear day it is the perfect spot to survey the whole of the surrounding countryside.

The less intrepid walker however, might be content to enjoy the views west across Troedyrhiw and south towards the twin valley settlements of Aberfan and Merthyr Vale. A tip near the mouth of the old Brazil Level, from where crystal clear and refreshing water now runs, offers the ideal position to enjoy the panorama. The impressive rocks of Graig y Pwll dominate this part of the valley and are in themselves well worthy of

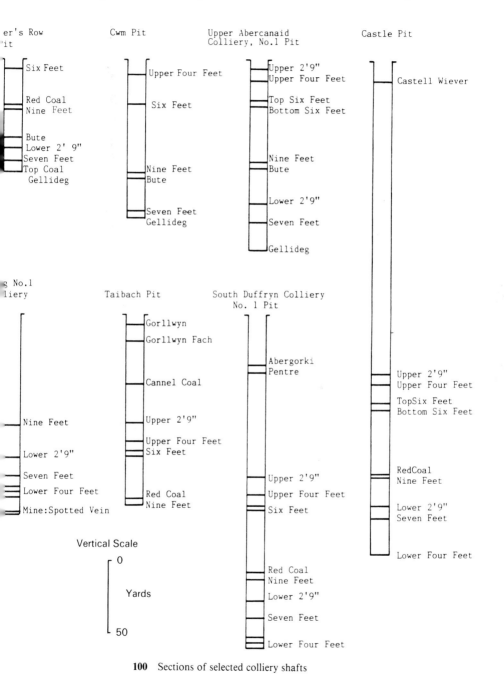

100   Sections of selected colliery shafts

129

101   South Duffryn Colliery, pit top and headgear

102   Winding engine-houses, South Duffryn Colliery, 1965

exploration. The visitor should take care, however, as the area is potentially dangerous with steep and slippery grass banks and much loose material which is easily dislodged.

Beneath these crags are the remains of the Troedyrhiw Lido, a place which once rang to the shouts and laughter of an earlier generation enjoying itself in the waters. There are, in fact, the remains of two pools, a circular paddling pool and a larger rectangular swimming pool, on the banks of which stands the concrete changing rooms. Sadly, both pools have been extensively vandalised. Frogs and small fish now swim in what water remains although small boys and girls partake of the occasional paddle with a degree of trepidation.

It is very difficult to reconcile the present dereliction with what prevailed on that summer day in 1934 when the newly painted doors and windows filled the now empty frames. Flags decorated the building and water lapped at the feet of those who sat around the pool's edge for the opening ceremony. A marquee had been erected and teas were served to all those who had come to celebrate this memorable occasion.

The land and materials for the pools were provided by Patrick Wyndham Murray Threipland, owner of quite a large area of land in Troedyrhiw, whilst the men of the village voluntarily gave their labour. In the years leading to the Second World War the lido was a big attraction for the local children. During the summer months and on Sunday evenings after chapel there was community hymn singing enjoyed by young and old, who thronged the mountainside around the pools.

103   Opening ceremony, Troedyrhiw Lido   *Mrs. H. Broad*

The valley sides generally are far less frequented today than in the past. The Pennant Sandstone is not now quarried to provide stone for house-building and men no longer have to carry bags of coal cut in the numerous small and unnamed levels which still pock-mark the hillside. As late as the 1950's the track past the Lido was used by those who lived at Penddeucae Farms and shopping was sometimes carried up the steep pathway which climbs Graig y Pwll. This precarious route was also taken on Saturday nights by men from Bedlinog who had earlier enjoyed a drink in one of the local pubs. Fewer adults derive pleasure from walking the mountainside, and the young do not indulge their childish pastimes there as perhaps their ancestors did. The gentler recreation of yesteryear has given way to the drama of the hang-gliders and the deafening din of the motorcycle rider.

Further south, below Troedyrhiw and on the valley floor itself, the outlines of the headgear of the Merthyr Vale Colliery remain one of the valley's last contacts with the heavy industry of its past. Now part of an extensive mining complex involving Deep Navigation Colliery at Treharris, Merthyr Vale was originally part of Nixon's Navigation Collieries and one of several pits sunk in the Taff and Cynon Valleys by John Nixon, an engineer and entrepreneur from County Durham. Nixon, in the true tradition of the nineteenth century industrialist, was a man for challenges. He had already overcome substantial obstacles in the sinking of collieries at Werfa and Deep Duffryn in the Aberdare Valley in order to build a successful and profitable group of collieries. Merthyr Vale was again to tax his resources, a fact clearly evidenced by the sinker's log which gives details of the difficulties involved.

The log book covers the period from August 20th. 1869 to Nov. 27th. 1873 in the sinking of the No. 1 Pit and from October 23rd. 1869 to Nov. 5th. 1874 in the sinking of No. 2 but sadly no indication is given of who was responsible for the entries. Generally it deals with the day-to-day progress of the workings and the selected extracts reproduced below can only hint at the qualities of courage, endeavour and perseverance which the sinkers must have possessed in large amounts to overcome the problems presented by the rock strata below the valley floor. For six years the men had to contend with the hardships and dangers of a succession of strata which held massive amounts of water and running sand. At the commencement, suspended side walls of timber were used to overcome the running silt but little ground had been won before the whole structure collapsed. Eventually John Nixon secured a supply of old rails from the Great Western Railway and together with large amounts of cast iron tubbing these were used to sink the pits through the treacherous strata.

1869.

August 20th. No. 1 Pit. Commenced to sink at 2 p.m. . . . . got water three feet from the surface.

August 24th. A. Rees got hurt by a fall of the tubbing.

132

August 28th. At 5.15 a.m. the surface of the ground began to give way on the south side of the pit. Sinking in fine running sand.

August 30th. The surface of the ground giving way so badly the men had to be brought out to strengthen the top framing.

August 31st. Stopped sinking at 7 a.m. and the pit allowed to fill with water.

September 2nd. Commenced pile driving at 5 p.m., the piles forty feet long and 12″ by 12″.

September 29th. The surface of ground on south-west side of pit going down so badly had all men out of pit timbering and filling on surface.

October 5th. Found the piles and surface of ground on the south side of pit going down and a great wash of gravel and sand coming up the centre of pit. Stopped sinking at 9 a.m., depth of sump thirty feet from surface and many segments of strong tubing broke and the pit quite out of circle. The pit was well stayed with timber and water allowed to rise.

October 22nd. Left off boring the hole on the south-west side of pit in hard rock. The pit was at this stage abandoned for the winter.

October 23rd. No. 2 Pit. Commenced an eight feet square pit on the site of the No. 2 Pit to go down through the gravel for the purpose of boring.

1870.

April 11th. Commenced to sink, very short of hands to begin with.

April 20th. We put in the ten feet shell centre of pit and sank as far as we could when at twenty-six feet from the surface a great wash of fine sand and water came away and we had to stop sinking.

August 19th. No. 1 Pit. A very severe wash took place on the south-west angle the ground giving away very bad indeed. We allowed the water at once to rise and commenced to drive the piles further down and to fill the ground around the pit where subsidence had taken place.

August 26th. Had to stop the sinking again owing to a great run and rush of water and sand on the south side. Paid off all the sinkers.

September 12th. Commenced to sink again at 7 a.m. found great difficulty in keeping the pumps in working order owing to the mud and silt at the bottom.

September 13th. Had to stop sinking again owing to wash and the ground subsiding so badly. We got as deep as thirty-eight feet from the surface but found by the morning the pit had silted up ten feet.

December 5th. Got into the bottom again when another wash came away on the south-east side of pit, the enginehouse, boilers and stack moving.

1871.

March 6th. No. 2 Pit. Sinkers struck work owing to reduction of wages by ten per cent.

March 13th. Sinkers and bankers commenced work at reduced rate of ten per cent.

September 5th. A stone fell from the side of No. 2 pit and caused Thomas Midcaffs death at 11.30 p.m.

December 5th. All going on right in the pit during the day up till 10.20 p.m.

105 Merthyr Vale Collery from Bell's Hill about 1880

106 Map of Merthyr Vale Colliery 1882

This map can be looked at in conjunction with figures 104 and 105, and several points are of interest:

1. When the map was made the village of Aberfan did not exist. There was a small coal mine (Perthygleison Pit) near the canal and a level entrance to these workings can still be seen near to the northern wall of Aberfan Cemetery

2. Near to the two farms of Aberfan Fawr and Aberfan Fach the row of cottages called Cwm Diflas still stand but are now called Perthygleison

3. The area of settlement on to the east of the Taff was called Ynys Owen (still the name of the telephone exchange of the area), and the rows of cottages marked are Nixonville, Crescent Street, Taff Street and Taff Street.

4. Where the river's course had to be altered is shown near to Ynysowen House

5. The ventilating machine was the patented Nixon reciprocating airpump and is visible as the well-buttressed building in Figure 105. to the right of the colliery headgear

6. The existence of a mine stone depot indicates that ironstone was being mined in considerable quantities at this time

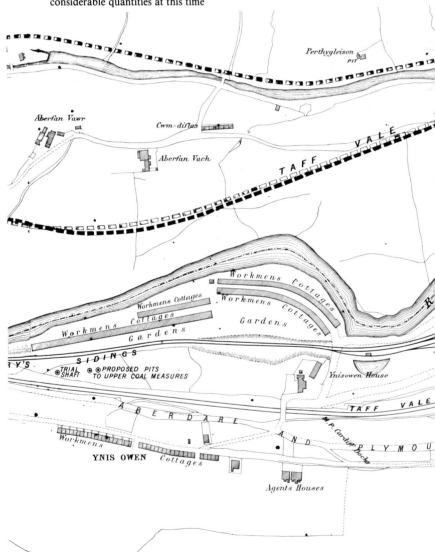

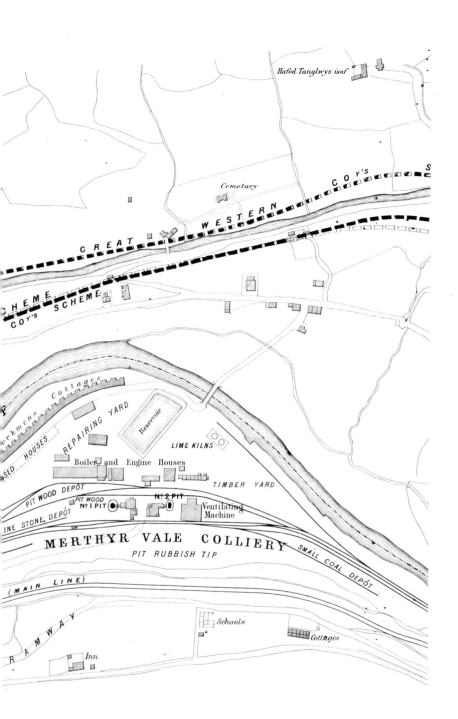

Hafod Tanglwys isaf

Cemetary

GREAT WESTERN COY'S S

SCHEME COY'S SCHEME

Workmens Cottages

DISUSED HOUSES

REPAIRING YARD

Reservoir

LIME KILNS

Boiler and Engine Houses

TIMBER YARD

PIT WOOD DEPÔT

PIT WOOD
Nº I PIT

Nº 2 PIT

LINE STONE DEPÔT

Ventilating
Machine

MERTHYR VALE COLLIERY

PIT RUBBISH TIP

SMALL COAL DEPÔT

(MAIN LINE)

TRAMWAY

Schools

Cottages

Inn

137

a hole that had misfired, two men James Chapel and John Jones were sent to clean it out by the chargeman and contrary to orders put a chisel in the hole and a striking hammer applied and while drilling the hole again the shot went off and the two named men were badly hurt and Edward Smith got a slight cut on his foot with a drill, the others including men that were in the bottom at the time with the above named men were unhurt.

1872.

June 6th. Name and dates put on big stack.

July 22nd. No. 1 Pit. All going on right in the pit up till 2 a.m. when three shots were to be fired and only two supposed to be lighted. John Longstaff the man appointed at the third hole, told the chargeman C. Thulron that he had not got his fuses lit. Consequently after two shots had gone off, Longstaff, E. Rees and Thulron descended to fire the one supposed not to be lit and when about nine feet from the bottom, the shot went off and John Longstaff received a slight blow on the eye and under his chin other men not harmed.

September 23rd. Bolt broke in the second cross collering from the bottom the collering fell away and caught David Price on the head and killed him on the spot.

October 29th. No. 2 Pit. Took the men away to No. 1 Pit at 2 p.m. not having plenty of men to keep both pits going.

November 25th. It was three o'clock before they got into the pit through Joseph Randel leaving his work and going up to the new public and getting tite.

1873.

January 1st. No. 1 Pit Very short handed and no chargemen at work.

January 6th. No. 2 Pit The men not in the pit at first through H. Payne getting a little too much drink.

March 24th. At 1.45 the bucket was on the lamp on the top of the pit and whether a shot had been left in the bucket or not I cannot tell but it exploded and shook the whole pit, blowing the bucket and the fire in all directions.

May 13th. Lightning conductor put up on big stack by John Jenkins.

May 24th. No. 1 Pit. All going on right stopped at 2 p.m. to attend supper at the Windsor Hotel.

June 21st. All went on well up till 4 p.m. when a piece of shuttering blew out. The men got out all right then a charge with three other sinkers went down in the box for to try to stop the water by putting in sheeting but they failed to get it in with the box, then they came to bank and took down the half stage and while putting on the piece of sheeting a second piece blew out which caught William Morris and knocked him down the pit among the water, this happened at 7.20 p.m. I went down myself at 7.55 p.m. and found that the poor fellow could not be got out by no means till the water was stopped. I lowered the stage to the top of the water and found about forty-five yards of water in I put down the grappeling irons with a plumbob on the end. I found the body and dragged the grappling-irons across the pit and got hold of him. I brought him with help to the top of the water put him in the bowk and brought him to bank at 12 o'clock midnight.

June 24th. Men off work to attend funeral.

July 15th. I sent some special rules away with Mr. Brown to get printed for the guidance of sinking Merthyr Vale Pit.

August 4th. All right in pit, charge taken away from Jas. Jones for neglect of duty.

August 22nd. I put up the rules for the guidence of the sinking.

September 17th. All right in bottom up till 7 a.m. a pump split and brought men out. At 4 p.m. I went down with davy lamp and tried the lamp at the holes that were open at the top of last tubbing and found a little gas coming out but no danger.

107   Nixon's Navigation Company Ltd.: Merthyr Vale Colliery, Officials 1897

Front Row, left to right. 1.David Williams, 2.Edwin Morgan, 3.   4.John Jones, 5.   6.Robert Snape (Manager), 7.H. E. Gray (Agent), 8.Tom Williams, 9.William Lewis, 10.   11.John Thomas, 12.John Parry
Middle Row, left to right. 1.   2.John Davies, 3.Rees Jones, 4.Evan Hopkins, 5.   Perkins, 6.J. O. Jones, 7.Phillip Parry, 8.Michael Jones, 9.B. M. Thomas, 10.Evan Thomas, 11.J. Gay, 12.   13.H. Williams, 14.C. Ascott, 15.
Back Row, left to right   1.Ben Bowen, 2.David Pugh, 3.R. Evans, 4.Evan Rees, 5.E. Taylor, 6.   7.William Bowen, 8.William Thomas, 9.Evan Jones, 10.David James. 11.John Rees.

108 Colliers about 1910

109 Colliery officials 1960

All other Photographs
Clive Thomas

1874.
January 22nd. No. 2 Pit. John Matthews caught stealing candles from pit top.
January 24th. John Matthews tried at Merthyr for the candle stealing found guilty and sent for twenty-one days to jail.
May 30th. Strike commenced.
June 11th. Men agreed to start work again but still too much water to get into No. 2.
July 24th. Griffiths the Contractor started on the pond today.
August 17th. Got men into the bottom after being out five weeks.

It was August of 1875 before the first coal was eventually raised from the Merthyr Vale Colliery, the No. 1 Pit having been sunk 425 yards to the Four Feet Seam and the No. 2 Pit 476 yards to the Nine Feet. Both shafts were deepened in 1930 to reach their present depths of 545 yards. Large quantities of high quality coal were mined in turn from the Four, Six and Nine Feet Seams with reserves existing now only in the Seven Feet and Gellideg Seams.

The mining of this coal has given employment to many thousands of men and boys during the last hundred years and brought an element of prosperity to the valley. It is however, the event of October 1966 which remains a blot on the history of the collieries' existence. Although no tips remain, the path the slide took is still discernible, if only because the vegetation, even twenty years afterwards, grows sparse and grudgingly.

The Aberfan Disaster remains a scar on the consciousness of all those who experienced its many and varied traumas and is a tragedy associated with a colliery which had been until the time of its occurrence, one of the most extensive, profitable and safe in the whole of the South Wales Coalfield.

References

Thomas, C. 'Industrial Development to 1918'. *Merthyr Tydfil—A Valley Community*, D. Brown and Sons, Cowbridge, in conjunction with Merthyr Tydfil Teachers' Centre Group, 1981.

Thomas, C. 'The Plymouth Ironworks' and 'A visit to the Remains of the Cyfarthfa Ironworks'. *Merthyr Historian*, Volume 1. Merthyr Tydfil Historical Society, 1976.

Owen, J. A. O. 'Merthyr Tydfil, Industrial Development 1870-1918', *Merthyr Historian*, Volume 2. Merthyr Tydfil Historical Society, 1978.

Morgan Rees, D. *Mines, Mills and Furnaces*. H.M.S.O., 1969.

Pedler, F. *History of the Hamlet of Gellideg*. Joseph Williams, Merthyr Tydfil, 1930.

Clarke, T. E. *A Guide to Merthyr Tydfil*, Merthyr Tydfil, 1848.

Davies, L. 'The Old Iron Bridge, Merthyr'. *Merthyr Historian*, Volume 2. Merthyr Tydfil Historical Society, 1978.

De La Beche, Sir Henry, *Report on the Sanitary Condition of Merthyr*, Health of Towns Commission, London, 1845.

Kay, William, *Report on the Sanitary Condition of Merthyr Tydfil*. Merthyr Tydfil, 1855.

Rammell, T. W., Report to the General Board of Health, London, 1850.

Strange, K., 'In Search of the Celestial Empire'—*Llafur* Vol. 3 No. 1., 1980.

Ginswick, J. Labour and the Poor in England and Wales 1849-51. Letters to the *Morning Chronicle* Volume 3. Frank Cass, 1983.

Jones, D. & Bainbridge, A., 'The Conquering of China', *Llafur* Vol. 2 No. 4, 1979.

Jones, D. 'Chartism at Merthyr, A Commentary on the Meetings of 1842', *Bulletin of the Board of Celtic Studies* Vol. XXIV, 1971.

Part Three:
Alien Plants In Our Midst

JACK EVANS

Our British flora is continually changing in response to the climate, the activities of man and other factors. If we have to decide whether or not a plant is native, our starting point must undoubtedly be the retreat of the vast ice sheets that covered Europe. As described in Section I, the Ice Age began about two million years ago. The ice advanced and retreated four times, the fourth major wave of glaciation lasting nearly 70,000 years.

At its furthest extent, the ice covered England and Wales as far south as the Bristol Channel to a depth of thousands of feet in places, and from our own area around Merthyr Tydfil one would have looked out over vast unbroken stretches of ice and glaciers as far as the eye could see.

At the end of the last advance of the ice, about 20,000 years ago, when the ice gradually withdrew, there would have been an increasing area of open and rock-strewn ground, with lakes of meltwater of varying sizes. Because of the scouring action of the ice, there was only the thinnest film of earth with very little humus. Plants that depended on deep rich soil found it hard to flourish, but there was room for those hardy species of modest and slow growth.

As the climate continued to improve, a greater variety of species began to move in from the south. Indeed, for part of the time the post-glacial climate was warmer than it is today. The flora was probably composed of a few hundred species of herbaceous annual and perennial plants, but as the new soil began to weather and form, a few species of trees and shrubs must have arrived; at first the pioneering birch, followed by pine, hazel and elm. So the growing numbers of species in our flora, estimated to be more than 5,000, all reached us in the post-glacial period, that is to say in the last 10-15,000 years. This period has seen the establishment of what can be termed the natives, together with the naturalisation of imported plants and aliens. This has been verified by many authorities using modern scientific methods, such as pollen analysis and various other historical dating techniques.

The greatest re-distributor of plants is man. No-one can move about the land without the probability of conveying seeds with them, and one can envisage over the centuries that many 'foreign' plants were introduced with successive waves of invaders. The Neolithic invaders were followed by the Early Bronze Age invasions of the 'Beaker' peoples, to be followed in turn

THE HISTORIC TÂF VALLEYS

SOME PLANTS OF ICE AGE BRITAIN

Pollen recovered from silt deposits laid down in glacial times in the few areas that remained vegetated, such as near the southern coasts and on the hills above the ice sheets, illustrate the range of dwarf trees and hardy species of plants that were able to survive and withstand the long cold winters. These were mainly small perennials, many of which are still common as weeds. Others, unable to compete with plants growing in the present mild climate, now grow mainly in marginal areas such as highland regions and around some of our coasts.

For botanical purposes, records of plant distribution are kept on a vice-county basis and in Wales these boundaries follow closely the political boundaries of the 13 counties as they were before the Local Government re-organisation of 1976. The counties where these native plants still occur is shown.

1. **Reticulate Willow**
   (*Salix reticulata*)
   Now found only in the Scottish mountains.

2. **Least Willow**
   (*Salix herbacea*)
   Once abundant in glacial times in the tundra vegetation. A scarce miniature shrub growing today on mountain cliffs in Brecs, Carms, Cards, Mer., Caerns.

3. **Purple Saxifrage**
   (*Saxifraga oppositifolia*)
   A mountain plant now found in Brecs, Mer., Caerns.

4. **Dwarf Birch**
   (*Betula nana*)
   A characteristic shrub of all periods when an Arctic flora existed in Britain. Does not occur in Wales but is found on some mountain moors in north England and Scotland

5. **Mountain Avens**
   (*Dryas octopetala*)
   Forced back to highland refuges by the spread of forest. Now found on mountain ledges in Caerns.

6. **Common Sorrel**
   (*Rumex acetosa*)
   Became especially widespread following the northward retreat of the ice-sheets. Frequent today in pastures of all Welsh counties.

7. **Black Sedge**
   (*Carex atrata*)
   Now a rarity of high mountains. Grows on mountain rocks in Caerns.

8. **Great Pond Sedge**
   (*Carex riparia*)
   Grew in the ponds of interglacial periods. Now found in marshes of most of our vice-counties.

9. **Curved Sedge**
   (*Carex maritima*)
   Now very rare, found only on the N.E. coasts of Britain.

10. **Hoary Whitlow Grass**
    (*Draba incarna*)
    An arctic alpine today found on mountain rocks in Caerns.

11. **Sea Plantain**
    (*Plantago maritima*)
    Was widespread throughout glacial times on ice-free ground. Occurs now on salt-marshes of all the Welsh counties.

12. **Spear-leaved Orache**
    (*Atriplex prostrata*)
    In glacial times grew on gravelly moraines and river shingles. A wayside weed found in waste places of all the vice-counties.

13. **Stinging nettle**
    (*Urtica dioicia*)
    During the glaciations occurred in tall herb "meadows". Very common on roadsides, cultivated and waste ground.

14. **Sea Pink or Thrift**
    (*Armeria maritima*)
    Though now mainly coastal and occasionally on mountains, Thrift was widespread in all glacial periods. Frequent on sea-cliffs around the Welsh coast.

15. **Annual Sea-Blite**
    (*Suaeda maritima*)
    Occurred in saline pools over frozen ground in inland districts during glacial times. Found today in salt marshes around the Welsh coast.

16. **Silverweed**
    (*Potentilla anserina*)
    Common in each glacial period. Now frequent in many habitats of all Welsh counties.

17. **Common Knot-grass**
    (*Polygonum aviculare*)
    Widespread in glacial times. Occurs frequently in cultivated ground and waste places of all Welsh counties.

18. **Creeping Buttercup**
    (*Ranunculus repens*)
    Flourished in the open ground of tundra during glacial times. Very common in cultivated ground and wet places of the Welsh counties.

by the late Bronze Age Celts, the Iron Age people and, in historic times, the invasions of the Romans, the Vikings and Danes, the Saxons and finally the Normans. All these made their respective introductions of new stocks of plants.

Apart from the accidental transport of alien plants, there was also the deliberate introduction of new species. Many of the human invaders brought seeds and roots of medicinal, culinary and fragrant herbs with which they had been familiar. Since the earliest of times, there was a widespread knowledge and understanding of the special virtues of various plants.

With the development of global traffic, intensive agricultural activities, drainage and land development of all sorts, the movement and origin of plants is continually widening. Apart from accidental introductions, selected seeds, flowers, shrubs and trees from all parts of the world are now deliberately planted in parks and gardens. Some escape into the surrounding countryside, where they occasionally succeed in establishing themselves, but the hazards are numerous. Some seeds lose their vitality, or the seedlings succumb to the new habitat or the differing climate. Often those that succeed in sustaining themselves become noxious and almost ineradicable weeds.

The flora of our country is thus a cosmopolitan assemblage of "natives" (by which we mean species that have been here before man arrived, or have immigrated without his aid by natural means of dispersal) and a large number of "aliens" (species that have been introduced by the intentional or unintentional agency of man) which have successfully established themselves over the centuries. Plant distribution is never at a standstill, but is constantly fluctuating, and even now new plants are being added yearly to the British flora, whilst at a slower rate others become extinct.

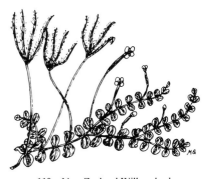

110 New Zealand Willow-herb

A small prostrate plant with white flowers and copper-coloured leaves demonstrates perfectly the vast and successful spreading of an alien plant. As its name implies, the **New Zealand Willowherb** (*Epilobium nerterioides*) is a native of New Zealand, where it occurs in open, damp places from the lowlands to rivers and streams at high altitudes. It was probably introduced into Britain as a pretty ground cover for rock gardens by someone unaware of how far willowherb seeds can travel. It was first recorded as a garden weed in 1904 near Edinburgh, where it had been known for several years. Twenty years later it really began to spread, and it was first found naturalised in Wales in 1930 near a stream at Pen-y-Gwryd in Snowdonia. The first record for South

Wales was in 1931, where it was noted as a garden weed at Rhiwbina, Cardiff, and the next was on a rubbish tip at Fochrhiw in 1944. The following year it was found naturalized on a wall at Cyfarthfa Park, Merthyr Tydfil. By 1963 the plant had spread to most of the Welsh counties. It was still found worthy of recording even in 1965, when it appeared at Ystradfellte and Penderyn. It continued to spread rapidly, and now it is quite at home on walls, rocks, paths and gardens in all parts of Britain, and can be seen everywhere firmly established on our hills, moorlands and mountains.

It is worth mentioning here another member of this family, **Rosebay Willowherb** (*Chaemaemerion angustifolium*) which is very common in our area and, although not an alien, it affords a striking instance of a native species that has been with us since late glacial times, but until this present century was regarded as a very uncommon plant. The Rev. C. A. Johns's 'Flowers of the Field'. published in 1911, has this entry for Rosebay, "A tall handsome species, 2-4 ft. high, not often met with in the wild state, but common in gardens where it is cultivated for the sake of its long racemes of handsome rose-coloured flowers. Caution should be used in introducing it into a small garden, as its roots creep extensively, and are very difficult to eradicate. Damp woods; rare, except as an escape." Nowadays, it is no longer found just in woodland clearings but on waste land, railway embankments and roadsides. The plant has a partiality for growth in burnt areas (thus the American name of Fireweed) and one of the main reasons for its massive spread was its appearance on bombed sites during the Second World War, 1939-45, where it flowered in profusion. When one considers that each flower spike can produce 80,000-100,000 parachute seeds, and that willow-herbs have the most efficient parachutes of all, giving the slowest fall of seeds, it becomes obvious why there should be this striking spread. Furthermore, there has been a marked increase in the frequency of heath and forest fires, whilst the extensive felling of woodlands in recent times has extended the habitats for this plant to colonise. But new habitats cannot be the whole story, and it is quite possible that this new vigour and adaptive capability has been brought about by some genetic change. There surely is no finer sight than a large spread of Rosebay Willowherb where the spikes of the reddish-purple flowers stand out boldly in any environment.

111   Rosebay Willow-herb

A plant far more attractive in appearance than New Zealand Willow Herb, and spreading quickly if not so dramatically, is the small purple-

112   Fairy Foxglove

flowered alpine from the mountains of southern Europe, the **Fairy Foxglove** (*Erinus alpinus*). It was first noted and recorded in our borough in Vaynor Quarries at Cefn Coed in May 1985, where it added vivid splashes of colour to many of the grey rock faces. The first record for Wales was near Troy Station on a wall at Troy House at Monmouth in 1916; it has since established itself at sixteen sites in eight of the old counties of Wales.

The plant is so popular in rock gardens, and the seeds are so very small and dust-like that it is not surprising that they have been wafted by the breeze to nearby walls and thence to other suitable habitats. Alternatively, they may have been transported in a more unorthodox and resourceful way. Richard Mabey, in his book 'The Flowering of Britain', published in 1980, mentions "This brilliant pink alpine has many fans, but none more devoted than the married couple who carry a stock of seeds with them on their travels round Britain, planting them out on any suitable limestone site". Perhaps the Vaynor Quarry has been on their seed dispersal itinerary, with a view to beautifying the bleak and dismal excavated hollows.

Many of our local streamsides and wet meadows glow with the yellow of the **Monkey Flower** (*Mimulus guttatus*). It is now so widespread in Britain that it is very difficult to realise that this plant first appeared as a garden escape in 1830, shortly after it was introduced from western North America.

113   Monkey flower

114   Musk

147

Monkey flower is a handsome plant with large two-lipped flowers blotched with red spots in the throat. The seeds are locally dispersed by wind, but probably the chief means of introduction to new areas has been by the seeds adhering to the feet and plumage of birds.

Musk (*Mimulus moschatus*) is another introduced plant of the same family. Although not quite so common in our area as the Monkey flower, it can nevertheless be found occasionally along streamsides and in moist habitats. It is smaller, covered all over with sticky hairs, and the all-yellow flowers are also much smaller than the Monkey flower. It was a favourite in old-fashioned cottage gardens and in window boxes because of the musk scent. Then, for some mysterious and inexplicable reason, during 1919-1920, the plant suddenly lost its perfume in most parts of the world.

The behaviour of plants can be exceedingly interesting, and the extra-ordinary sensitivity of the Monkey flower is worth a mention. The pistil has a two-lobed stigma, the lips of which close when touched, and will later re-open. But if you dust the lips with the flower's own pollen, they will close upon it and remain shut. If, on the other hand, you dust the lips with a small grain of sand or pollen from another species, they open again shortly afterwards. Kill some of its own pollen (by heating, for instance) and one finds that the plants can even discriminate between live and dead pollen, as with the latter the lobes are wide open a little after being dusted. Obviously, the lips of the stigma respond to contact of any kind, but in some way, possibly chemical, they have a very selective response to the living pollen.

A striking example of a herbaceous border plant, very popular in gardens of the past, but which has now become successfully established in un-cultivated areas, is **Japanese Knotweed** (*Reynoutria japonica*). It was better known as *Polygonum cuspidatum*, but taxonomists have a habit of frequently changing the names. This tall, vigorous shrub is very common alongside streams and on our waste grounds, and is a beautiful sight in full bloom, with its feathery white masses of

115   Japanese Knotweed

creamy flowers. A very fine stand of it can be seen on the western bank of the river on the south side of the Technical College Car Park bridge. Once established, it requires hard sweated labour to eradicate, and it has become a widespread pest by completely dominating certain areas at the expense of all other smaller plants.

It was introduced into gardens from Japan in 1825, and thereafter in horticultural journals of the time it was described as "a plant of sterling merit, now becoming quite common, and is undoubtedly one of the finest herbaceous plants in cultivation". The writer of this must have been a gardening sadist, as over the years it would have ruined many a garden since it spreads by means of its very tough and stout rhizomes. It is now one of only two plants whose introduction into the British countryside is prohibited.

Ivy-leaved toadflax (*Cymbalaria muralis*) was introduced as a garden

116   Ivy-Leaved Toadflax

plant from Southern Europe, probably about the early part of the 1600's, and is now a common plant which has spread far and wide on old walls throughout Britain. It is particularly luxuriant on many of our old walls cemented with lime mortar. One of its popular names, Mother of Thousands, acknowledges this roving and quickgrowing habit. This is made possible by an interesting method of multiplication. The fruits containing the seeds are borne on long stalks which react to light in such a way as to put the capsule into dark cracks where the seeds can germinate. The pretty bluish snapdragon-like flowers are easily recognised.

Alongside many of our local streams, riversides and bare wet places can be seen a tall robust plant with a brittle hollow stem, sometimes five feet or more, and bearing pale purple and white dangling slipper-shaped flowers. It is **Himalayan Balsam** (*Impatiens glandulifera*) and, as its name implies, is a native of the Himalayas. It was first introduced into a garden in 1839 and its relatively recent naturalisation is mostly alongside river banks. The reason why it should be restricted to the river-side habitat is quite strange, as it is so easy to cultivate in ordinary garden soil. It has become colonised in most parts of the British Isles and dense thickets of it grow on the banks of the River Wye. Two of the common names for the plant are Policeman's Helmet and Touch-me-not, the latter referring to the mechanism of the ripe fruit, which certainly explodes impatiently when touched. This is quite an effective method of spreading seed over a short area of ground, and much further afield, when the

117   Himalayan Balsam

149

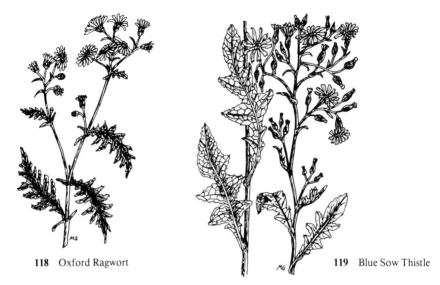

118 Oxford Ragwort   **119** Blue Sow Thistle

seeds are shot on to the water and float, to be washed up on a fresh site downstream.

An interesting garden escape which is now quite common in our area is the **Oxford Ragwort** (*Senecio squalidus*) with yellow daisy-like flowers about an inch across. A native of Sicily, where the plant grew freely on the volcanic ash from Mount Etna, it was grown in the Oxford Botanic Gardens in the 17th century. Its windborne seeds started escaping at the end of the 18th century, when it was noted on some of the old walls in Oxford. With the increasing network of railway tracks all over the country, it found the rubble foundations much to its liking, and began to colonise many parts. The bombed sites of the Second World War provided ground conditions very similar to those of Mount Etna, and these became carpeted with yellow masses of flowers. At the present time it is found in most parts of the

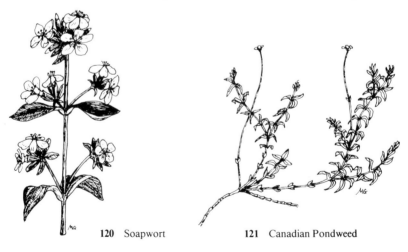

120 Soapwort   **121** Canadian Pondweed

country, where it is firmly established and still spreading. Although closely related to the **Common Ragwort** (*Senecio jacobeae*), that poisonous nuisance to livestock, the Oxford can be recognised by the short black tips on the green sepals.

A plant well worth a mention and quite uncommon in our locality is the **Blue Sowthistle** (*Cicerbita plumieri*). Its only station here seems to be an area in the Gurnos. It is a garden escape, introduced into this country from the Caucasus and, although an attractive plant with its blue chicory-like flowers against a background of bluish-green foliage, it would be very invasive in cultivation, as it spreads rapidly by means of underground stems. Someone in the Gurnos has painfully discovered this, and helped it over the garden wall, to flourish in the wild.

Soapwort (*Saponaria officinalis*), a stout herbaceous perennial, two to three feet high, derives its name from the fact that the leaves produce a soapy lather when rubbed with water. Consequently, it was frequently used in the fulling mills for washing wool. It may have been a deliberate introduction by our local fullers and, once naturalized, it remains firmly established by reason of its creeping underground stems. The plant is still used as a cleansing agent for very old and delicate fabrics where the brilliance and depth of the ancient fibres from which they were woven needs to be restored. Such other vernacular names as Soaproot, Latherwort, Fuller's Herb and Crow Soap bear evidence of the use to which this plant was put. The plant was introduced into Britain in the sixteenth century, although the Romans were aware of its value and it seems likely that they also grew it during their period of occupation.

Most people are familiar with **Canadian waterweed** (*Elodea canadensis*), particularly those who grow it in aquaria or garden ponds as a very good oxygenator for the water. It was introduced into Britain somewhere between 1830 and 1840 from North America, and spread so rapidly both here and later on the continent of Europe that it threatened to block waterways and ditches. Fortunately, after a peak of rapid and alarming growth, the impetus to spread began to decline, until today it is a reasonably common plant to be found in most areas. All the British plants are female, and as no seeds are set they must rely solely on vegetative reproduction to spread.

The bright blue flowers of the speedwell family are well known, particularly **Germander Speedwell** (*Veronica chaemaedrys*) known locally as Bull's Eye. This is a native flower and quite common; but perhaps the most commonly occurring variety is the **Common Field Speedwell** or **Buxbaum's Speedwell**

122   Buxbaum's Speedwell

(*Veronica persica*), a low sprawling hairy annual with sky-blue flowers. It is a weed of cultivation, and flourishes profusely in gardens and on arable land. It is difficult to realise that it is a relatively recent arrival in Britain from western Asia. The flower was first noted in Berkshire in 1825, since when it has managed to spread over the whole of the country.

A tall plant of from one to two feet, found very occasionally growing in arable land and waste places and bearing clusters of creamy white flowers,

123   Hoary Cress or Pepper Cress   124   Pineappleweed or Rayless Mayweed

is the **Pepper Cress** or **Thanet Cress** (*Cardaria draba*). Because the leaves bear numerous hairs, it is also called Hoary Cress. The seeds contained in the heart-shaped pods were formerly ground as a substitute for pepper— thus the name. It is a recently spread plant, first appearing in the early part of the 18th century. Apparently it was introduced from the Continent by fever-stricken soldiers being brought back home on mattresses stuffed with hay, which were eventually sold to a Thanet farmer who ploughed it in for manure. The cress subsequently appeared, presumably from seeds mixed with the hay, and from this accidental beginning it has now spread to all parts of the country.

Rayless Mayweed (*Matricaria matricarioides*) is found growing in many of our waste places, farmyards, cultivated ground and along the sides of quiet lanes. It was first recorded in Britain in 1871 and is now widely dispersed. It is a native of Oregon, and when the leaves are bruised or crushed they smell of apple or pineapple, which accounts for its other popular name, Pineapple Weed.

Anyone who has grown **Montbretia** (*Crocosmia x crocosmiflora*) in a garden border will have experienced how quickly it spreads and takes over all the open spaces. Although an attractive plant, with its spikes of orange

125 Montbretia

126 Buddleia

flowers, this invasive habit has resulted in large chunks being thrown out. The same process of vigorous growth happens in the wild, and one comes across it in many different habitats, alongside walls and on the fringe of woodlands. Interestingly enough, this flower did not exist before the late 1870's when a successful cross between two South African irises was made by a French nurseryman.

One of the most familiar and decorative plants to colonise some of our waste areas is the very common shrub **Buddleia** (*Buddleia davidii*). Open spaces created in redevelopment areas are rapidly colonized by the shrub, and in recent years it has certainly become a 'native' of these waste places. The plant is, of course, a garden escape and is in fact a Chinese shrub discovered by a European botanist in 1887. The long purple inflorescences that appear in summer are particularly attractive to butterflies, and consequently it is sometimes called the "butterfly bush".

Another two shrubs from the garden that are now completely at home in the wild are the **Cotoneasters** (*C. microphyllum*), which comes from the Himalayas, and *C. horizontalis*, from China, both introduced in the last century. They are attractive plants loaded with red berries in the autumn, the former an evergreen shrub with wide-spreading branches and the latter deciduous with the branches arranged in an attractive herring-bone fashion. These are particularly appealing when they are seen growing against bare rock faces as, for instance, at the old Dolygaer railway station.

A naturalised shrub with large white berries, the **Snowberry** (*Symphoricarpus rivularis*) can be found in many parts of the locality. It is a native of North America and was introduced about 1817 for the prized white fruits, useful for autumn and winter floral arrangements. As these shrubs suckered freely, they were also used frequently for low hedges.

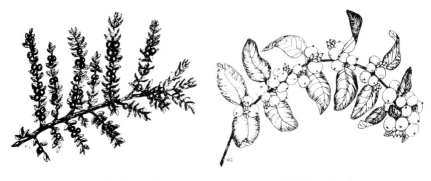

127 Cotoneaster horizontalis   128 Snowberry

Almost everyone would recognise the **Rhododendron**, and the story of the plant explorers who collected seed and plants of different species from China, Tibet, Nepal and Burma is a fascinating one. There are about 900 species, but *R. ponticum*, with its dark glossy leaves and mauve flowers has become naturalized and is a noxious weed of some of our woodlands. It was introduced from Spain and Portugal in 1763 and was probably the first rhododendron seen in this country. Given an acid soil, which is a prime necessity for the whole family, they can spread both vegetatively and by seedlings. In some parts of the country they are becoming a menace to horticulture and forestry because of their resistance to control by herbicides.

The **Great Periwinkle** (*Vinca major*) with its large and attractive sky-blue flowers, is an escaped garden plant which can be seen trailing rampantly in some of our woodlands and thickets. Alongside the Taf Fawr in the cemetery at Cefn Coed, the woodland floor is thickly carpeted with its glossy and dark green leaves. Perhaps there was a good reason for its introduction to this country, because a medical manuscript of the fourteenth century says that, powdered with earthworms and eaten with food, it induces love between husband and wife.

The pale pink flowers of the **Winter Heliotrope** (*Petasites fragrans*) which now scent some of our river banks in February and March, were introduced

129 Rhododendron   130 Greater Periwinkle

131   Winter Heliotrope

132   Pearly Everlasting

into this country from Southern Europe during the early part of the last century. Although similar to the much more common **Butterbur** (*Petasites hybridus*), it can be distinguished by its shorter and much smaller leaves.

Pearly Everlasting (*Anaphalis magaritacea*) with its whitish woolly leaves and yellow flowerheads, has colonised many of our local industrial tips and old railway tracks in a relatively short time. It was introduced very early as a rockery plant from North America, and in 1696 Edward Llwyd found it growing in Monmouthshire for at least 12 miles alongside parts of the Rhymney River.

133   Red Valerian

A later introduction from southern Europe in the 16th century was **Red Valerian** (*Centranthus ruber*) which can now be found growing on banks, cliffs and walls. It is a perennial plant and its bluish-green smooth leaves persist throughout the year. The very young leaves are eaten in salads in France and Italy.

A striking example of how plants can remain localised for a lengthy period and then begin to spread, is demonstrated by the **Caper Spurge** (*Euphorbia lathyris*) which suddenly appeared in the author's garden at Cefn Coed about 12 years ago. This biennial plant which can grow to three or four feet tall, is something of a nuisance in gardens, as it sows itself in abundance, but it has such an architectural charm that some plants can be carefully sited and left to grow. It is a native of woodlands in southern

155

Europe and was cultivated in herb gardens as a purgative. Gerard wrote in his 17th century Herball that it "is a strong medicine to open the bellie".

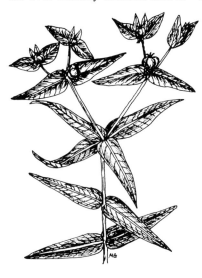

The seeds were sometimes used in place of capers for flavouring in pickles and sauces, but the practice was discontinued because of the occasional harmful effects. The only plants recorded as occurring wild in Glamorgan are mostly near the coast, but in 1985, some were noted in a woodland about half a mile from the Cefn Coed site. Although the seeds spread by an explosive mechanism and a few plants have appeared in a neighbour's garden, they would have had to be nuclear-powered to travel such a distance to the woodland. The only seemingly rational explanation is that they have been transported on the feet of birds.

134 Caper Spurge

A showy plant introduced from North America into our gardens in the 19th century, and now frequently common on our many industrial waste tips is the **Evening Primrose** (*Oenothera biennis*). Its successful spread can be attributed to the very large number of seeds produced, about 30,000 to each plant.

Two cultivated plants that have found suitable habitats on old walls are the **Biting Stonecrop** (*Sedum acre*) and the daisy-like **Blue Fleabane** (*Erigeron acer*). The former is also called Bittercress or Wall-pepper because of its succulent bitter leaves. It has what must be one of the longest

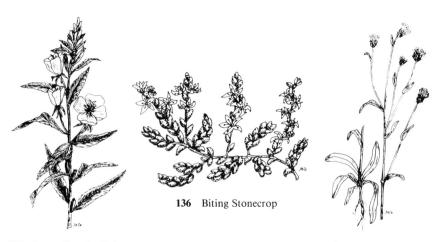

136 Biting Stonecrop

135 Lesser Evening Primrose

137 Blue Fleabane

and strangest of English names, "Welcome-home-husband-though-never-so-drunk". **Canadian Fleabane** (*Erigeron canadensis*), common in waste places, is a North American weed which has actually spread from there around most of the globe. It has been with us for nearly three centuries, being first recorded at a site near London.

Medicinal Plants

It has been mentioned previously that some of our now well-established plants came straight from the herb gardens. Herbs are the oldest kind of medicine in the world, and they were widely grown for healing and culinary purposes long before the days of doctors, veterinary surgeons, chemists' shops and supermarkets. Herbalism, defined as the art of healing by the use of non-poisonous herbs, can be traced back through the civilisations of Rome, Greece, Assyria and Babylon, to Sumerian times.

As a matter of fact, the earlier botanists studied plants from scarcely anything but their medicinal attributes, and herb gardens were cultivated on a large scale. It was both natural and sensible that earlier generations, having found in plants the source of their food supply when in health, should again turn to nature when their bodily functions went amiss.

They were not equipped with the knowledge we possess today, a knowledge which enabled us to extract a variety of substances from the earth, and by very complex processes produce synthetic drugs. Their medicine had to be as obvious and simple as their food.

They were certainly not wrong in following their instincts, for in various parts of selected plants they found effective remedies for their several ailments.

But study of herbs and their curative effects sometimes resulted in mythical concoctions and a great amount of charlatanism. In Shakespeare's "Macbeth", for instance, we read of such medicines as 'scale of dragon', 'tooth of wolf', 'gall of goat', 'slips of yew', 'root of hemlock digg'd i' the dark', and so forth. Today, our chief practical aim in growing garden herbs is to supply flavourings for the kitchen and possibly aromas to delight our sense of smell.

The subject of medicinal herbs holds a mysterious fascination for many people, and, to digress for a moment, many are perhaps conversant with the legend of the Lady of Llyn-y-Fan Fach, or the Lady of the Lake. For those who are not acquainted with the rich store of Welsh folklore, myth and legend, or who have not visited the superb, majestic and mystical Llyn-y-Fan Fach in the Black Mountain of Carmarthenshire, the story is worth recounting. This version comes from an early 19th century rendering, translated from the Welsh.

138   Llyn-y-Fan-Fach in the Black Mountain near Llanddeusant, Dyfed   *Graham Bird*

"Towards the close of the twelfth century, a widowed woman and her son lived at the farmhouse of Blaensawdde near the village of Llanddeusant. The son looked after the cattle, which he grazed on the slopes of the Black Mountain, at his favourite place near the small lake of Llyn-y-Fan Fach.

One day, whilst walking alongside the lake, to his great astonishment he saw, sitting on the calm waters and combing her hair, one of the most beautiful maidens that mortal eyes had ever seen. Bewildered by a feeling of love and admiration for the lady he saw before him, he held out his hand to offer some of the barley bread and cheese which was his food for the day. But she gently refused his offer, saying

"Cras dy fara!
Nid hawdd fy nala"
"Hard baked is thy bread!
'Tis not easy to catch me",

and immediately disappeared under the water.

The love-stricken youth returned to his mother and related his story. She advised him to try again, but this time making an offer of unbaked bread.

Early the next morning the youth was waiting at the lakeside, seemingly in vain. Many hours had passed, when suddenly he noticed some of his cattle were in danger on the precipitous slope on the opposite side of the lake. He was hurrying to save them, when the maiden suddenly appeared above the lake surface looking more beautiful and desirable than before. He held out his offering of unbaked bread and pledged his eternal love, but she again refused his offer, saying

"Laith dy fara!
Ti ni fynna".
"Unbaked is thy bread!
I will not have thee".

But she smiled as she again disappeared beneath the waters, softening his despair, and raising his hopes. When he returned home, his mother suggested a gift of lightly baked bread. Very early the following day, he was feverishly waiting by the lakeside for the reappearance of the lovely maiden. Day was turning into night when, to his astonishment, he saw some of the cattle walking on the surface of the lake, and almost immediately they were followed by the maiden, looking even lovelier than ever.

Her smile encouraged him to take her hand, and she did not refuse his gift of bread or his protestations of love. She consented to become his bride on condition that she would leave him if he struck her three times without cause;

"Tri ergyd diachos"
Three causeless blows.

He readily agreed to this condition, and would have consented to any other stipulation, but to his consternation, she suddenly disappeared. Just as, in his grief, he was considering throwing himself into the lake after her, there emerged out of the water two most beautiful ladies, accompanied by a hoary man of great stature. The man addressed the youth, saying he would allow his daughter to marry a mortal if the young man could tell which of the two maidens she was. This was no easy task, as they looked alike, and the young man was unable to see any difference until one of the maidens placed her foot slightly forward as a sign to him, and he quickly made the correct choice. Her father offered a dowry of as many animals as his daughter could count in one breath and, counting rapidly in fives, the goats, cattle, sheep and horses came out of the lake accordingly.

And so the marriage took place. The young couple lived at a farm called Esgair Llaethdy (Ref. 786 296) near the village of Myddfai, where they lived in prosperity and happiness, and where she bore three sons.

One day, the husband asked his wife to fetch a horse from the fields so that they could attend a local christening, while he promised to collect her gloves from the house. Finding his wife had not gone, he tapped her playfully on the shoulder, saying "dos, dos" (go, go). She reminded him of the one condition she had made when she married him, and warned him to be more cautious in the future.

On another occasion, when they were together at a wedding, the wife began to cry and sob. Her husband touched her rather roughly on the shoulder to enquire the cause of the weeping, when she said, "Now people are entering into trouble, and your troubles are likely to commence as you have the second time struck me without cause". The husband vowed to be more careful in the future. The years passed, and the three sons grew to become clever young men.

It happened that one day the couple were at a funeral where, amidst the mourning and grief, the Lady became gay and joyful. This so shocked the husband that he shook her, saying "Hush, hush, don't laugh!" She replied that the dead person had left this troubled life, and added "the last blow has been struck, our marriage contract is broken and at an end! Farewell." Then she went back to Esgair Llaethdy, where she called her cattle and other stock together, each by name, and set off towards the lake, six miles distant. Even a small black calf which had been slaughtered and hung on a hook became alive and followed her, as did the four oxen ploughing in the fields. What became of the frightened ploughman or the distraught and ruined husband is not handed down in the legend.

But of the sons, it is stated that they often wandered by the lake and its vicinity, hoping that they would see their mother. In one of their rambles it happened at a place near Dol Howell at the Mountain Gate still called "Llidead y Meddygon", the Physicians' Gate, the mother appeared suddenly to the eldest son Rhiwallon. She told him that his mission on earth was to be a benefactor of mankind by relieving them of pain and misery through healing of all diseases. To this end, she supplied him with a bag full of prescriptions and instructions for the preservation of health. She prophesied that he and his family would become for many generations the most skilful physicians in the country.

On several occasions she met her sons near the banks of the lake, and once she accompanied them on their return to their home as far as a place called "Pant-y-Meddygon" the Dingle of the Physicians, where she pointed out to them the various plants which grew there and their medicinal qualities and virtues. The knowledge she imparted to them, together with their unrivalled skill, soon caused them to attain great celebrity.

Resulting from this folk story, a body of legends was built around the Physicians of Myddfai, and their fame soon spread, with their services in demand throughout Wales.

Rhys Gryg, who was Lord of Llandovery and Dynevor, appointed Rhiwallon a mediciner of the royal court and his domestic physician. Rhiwallon was assisted in this office by his three sons, Gruffydd, Cadwgan and Einion. Under his patronage the Physicians collected the medicinal cures and remedies of the preceding ages and, together with prescriptions derived from their own healing skills, "caused a record of their skill to be committed to writing, lest no one be found after them so endowed with the requisite knowledge as they were".

Today, two farms near the village of Myddfai are still called "Llwyn Ifan Feddyg" (The Grove of Evan the Physician) and "Llwyn Meredydd Feddyg". The descendants of this family practised medicine in the country without a break until the last lineal descendant died in 1743. A tombstone

139 Myddfai Church   *Jack Evans*

140   The Tombstone inside the Porch of Myddfai Church   *Jack Evans*

fixed against the west end of Myddfai Church inside the porch, records the death in 1719 of David Jones of Mothvey, Surgeon, a reputed descendant, and of his surgeon son in 1739. The inscription reads:—Here / Lieth the Body of Mr. / David Jones of Mothvey, / Surgeon, who was an / honest, charitable and skillfull / man. He died Septm^r ye 14th / Anno Dom. 1719 / aged 61. John Jones, Surgeon / eldest son of the said / David Jones departed / this life the 25th of November / 1739 in the 44th yeare of his / age and also lyes interred / hereunder. Another descendant became Bishop of Llandaff in the 17th century. The late Dr. C. Rice Williams, M.D., of Aberystwyth, who died aged 85 years in 1842, seems to have been the last of the Physicians of Myddfai.

The physicians made a collection of recipes, many traced back to the times of Howel Dda and much earlier, and put them in writing for the first time. The original manuscript is now to be found in the British Museum, but the most important copy known to exist is the Red Book version at Jesus College, Oxford. John Pughe, FRCS, translated it from the Welsh in 1861 for the Welsh Manuscript Society.

Extracts from this text are included here to embellish some of the plant descriptions and to provide an insight into the art of healing as practised from the Middle Ages onwards. Mainly, if not wholly, it was performed by means of herbs. The contrast with the methods of our own times is quite dramatic, but perhaps readers a few centuries hence will consider the present-day remedies for our diverse ailments just as strange, baffling and sometimes bizarre as those of the past are to us.

Another famous work, by Nicholas Culpeper, was first published in 1653 and entitled "The Complete Herbal and English Physician wherein several hundred herbs with a Display of their Medicinal and Occult Properties are physically applied to the cure of all Disorders Incident to Mankind". As can be seen by the title, astrology had one of its most zealous advocates in Culpeper, and this work remained for some two hundred years one of the most popular guides to herbal medicine in the British Isles. Some of the remedies are also included here to elaborate the description of the appropriate herb.

The Romans introduced many medicinal plants to cope with their many physical ailments, among them **Ground Elder** (*Aegopodium podagraria*), **Fennel** (*Foeniculum vulgare*) and **Wormwood** (*Artemisia absinthium*). Ground elder, prized by them as a medicinal herb and a pot herb, must have occasioned more expletives and sweated labour among local gardeners than any other pernicious weed. A member of the umbelliferae, it spreads in all directions with exceptional rapidity by means of its underground stems, and the roots can regenerate from small fragments, making any assault on the weed unlikely to succeed. Furthermore, it is difficult to eradicate by chemical methods as no selective herbicide has yet been found that has more than a temporary effect. John Gerard, the 16th century herbalist, and the writer of the famous 'Herball' wrote of it "It groweth of it selfe in gardens,

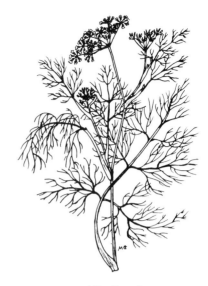

141 Ground Elder   **142** Fennel

without setting or sowing and it is one so fruitful in his increase that where it hath once taken roote, it will hardly be gotten out again, spoiling and getting every yeere more ground, to the annoying of better herbes''. Another common name for this plant is **Goutweed**, and apart from its use as an aromatic pot herb, it was employed as a valuable remedy for this complaint. Culpeper says of it, ''Saturn is the ruler of this plant. It is probable it took the name of gout-herb from its peculiar virtues in healing the cold gout and sciatica, as it hath been found by experiments to be a most admirable remedy for these disorders; as also joint aches and other cold disorders. It is even affirmed that the very carrying of it about in the pocket will defend the bearer from any attack of the aforesaid complaint''.

Another culinary umbelliferous herb that has escaped from cultivation is **Fennel**, and although not common growing wild in our area, it occurs in a few waste places. It is an aromatic plant with finely divided leaves and yellow flowers, that was used, and still is, as a flavouring and for its succulent edible shoots. In medieval times fennel was regarded as a preventive against witchcraft, and was hung above doors at midsummer. Fennel was frequently used in recipes in 'The Physicians of Myddfai', and the following are two of them:

''To promote the secretion of Urine, the growth of Flesh, Skin and Bones
Take a handful of red roses, spring water, the juice of celandine, honey, juice of hemlock, fennel, tutsan, burdock, a spoonful of a suckling child's urine, and red wine, mix these ingredients together, warm them a little, then remove from the fire, strain and keep. Let this be applied to a sloughing wound and it will cleanse and heal it.

163

To make an Eye Salve

Take the juice of fennel root, celandine, lesser celandine, sow's lard, honey, a little vinegar, an eel's blood and a cock's gall, letting them stand in a brass vessel till an efflorescence takes place. This has restored sight to those who had quite lost it.''

Wormwood is a highly scented escape from the herb garden, and is a grey-foliaged hairy perennial with yellow flower heads. It is frequently found growing on waste ground. The plant was formerly used as a tonic and as a cure for intestinal worms, hence the name. It is now used for making vermouth and absinthe, a very strong alcoholic drink. A recipe as an "Ointment for general use" appears in the 'Physicians of Myddfai':

"take a gander's fat, the fat of a male cat, a red boar's fat, three drams of blue wax, watercress, wormwood, the red strawberry plant and primrose, boil them in pure spring water, and when boiled stuff a gander with them, and roast them from a distance from the fire, the grease issuing from it should be carefully kept in a pot. It is a valuable ointment for all kinds of ache in a man's body and is like one that was formerly made by Hippocrates. It is proved.''

At the end of many of these fantastic remedies, the Physicians wrote with firm assurance "It is proved" with no doubt, the object of fortifying a faith

143 Wormwood

in the healing power of the concoction. The magic probably worked because faith is a very powerful ally in the healing process. We are neither more nor less gullible than these patients of a few centuries ago. Heavily laden shelves in modern chemists' shops abound with proven cures for almost every known ailment, so the only change has been the vogue.

Culpeper had this to say about Wormwood: "This is a martial herb and is governed by Mars. The tops with the flowers on them, dried and powdered are good against agues, and have the same virtues with wormseed in killing worms. It is admirable against surfeits. It not only cures pain of the stomach, weakness, indigestion, want of appetite, vomiting and loathing, but hard swellings of the belly. This with rosemary, saffron and turmeric root, infused in rhenish wine, is a cure for the jaundice, and brings down the menses.''

A plant very similar in appearance to Wormwood and closely related to it is **Mugwort** (*Artemisia vulgaris*), found in hedgerows, waysides and particularly in waste places. Mugwort was used as an aromatic culinary herb and was occasionally used as a substitute for tea when this beverage was very expensive. It was also regarded as a worm dispeller, and all Artemisias

144 Mugwort

145 Comfrey

contain small quantities of a substance called Santonin which does remove worms, but which is a hallucinogen if taken in overdose, causing objects to appear first as blue and then slowly changing to yellow.

Comfrey (*Symphytum officinale*), a large perennial herb occasionally found in damp places, especially alongside some of our streams, has a host of country names, including Knitbone, Bruisewort, Boneset, indicating some of the uses to which some of our forefathers put it. The plant produces yellowish, bluish or purplish-white flowers in May and June, all on one side of the plant. It was widely cultivated in cottage gardens because of its enormous reputation as a wound healer and as an aid in the mending of fractures. There is a clear medical basis for this. The plant is a very rich source of a substance called allantoin, which stimulates cell division and greatly speeds up the healing process by the proliferation of new cells.

Culpeper used this herb in one of his remedies. "This is a herb of Saturn under the sign of Capricorn, cold, dry and earthy in quality. The root being outwardly applied, helpeth fresh wounds or cuts immediately, being bruised and laid thereunto; and is especial good for ruptures and broken bones; yea, it is said to be so powerful to consolidate and knit together that, if they are boiled with dis-severed pieces of flesh in a pot it will join them together again. The roots of comfrey taken fresh, beaten small, and spread upon leather, and laid upon any place troubled with the gout, do presently give ease of the pain; and applied in the same manner, give ease to pained joints, and profit very much for running and moist ulcers, gangrenes, mortifications and the like, for which it hath by often experience been found helpful.''

A favoured plant growing in herb gardens of past generations was the **Feverfew** (*Chrysanthemum parthenium*), a name which referred to the supposed virtue of its ability to reduce various fevers. This highly aromatic plant with many daisy-like flowerheads, was introduced into the country from S.E. Europe, and is found growing on old walls and in waste places. The country folk made and still make an infusion of the leaves, which was taken as a cure for headaches, just as people nowadays take aspirin. The Physicians of Myddfai made use of it in the following way:

"*A Healing Ointment for Bruises*
Take feverfew, ribwort plantain, garden sage and bugle, equal parts of each, pound them well and boil in unsalted May butter, then express through a fine linen, and keep in a box. Anoint the disease therewith and it will cure it. If there be dead flesh therein, take some sloes, or sulphate of copper, or red precipitate of mercury in powder, and mix with some of the ointment, then it will destroy the dead flesh and promote the healing of the sore."

Gerard gave as its virtues "Feverfew dried and made into pouder, and two drams of it taken with hony or sweet wine, purgeth by siege melancholy and flegme; wherefore it is very good for them that are giddie in the head, or which have the turning called Vertigo, that is, a swimming and turning in the head. Also it is good for such as be melancholike, sad, pensive and without speech."

Closely related to feverfew, and found growing locally by roadsides and waysides is **Tansy** (*Chrysanthemum vulgare*), a tall flower with bunches of yellow, flat button-like flowers and fern-like leaves. The leaves when crushed are powerfully aromatic. It was popular as a flavouring herb and also to destroy or expel intestinal worms. John Gerard explains some of the

146   Feverfew   **147**   Tansy

uses of Tansy in his 17th century "Herball". "In the Springtime are made with the leaves here of newly sprung up, and with eggs, cakes of Tansies, which be pleasant in taste, and good for the stomacke. For if any bad tumours cleave there unto, it doth perfectly concot them, and scowre them downewards." Culpeper recommends it for many ailments, and for women wanting to give birth. "this herb, bruised and applied to the navel, stays miscarriages; I know no herb like it for that use; boiled in ordinary beer and the decoction drank, does the like; and if her womb be not as she would have it, this decoction will make it so. Let those women that desire children love this herb, it is their best companion, the husband excepted."

The Physicians of Myddfai saw in Tansy virtues

"*For all Complaints of the Eyes Particularly Opacities*"

Take wild or garden tansy, and boil well in white wine till the virtue of the herb is extracted; then remove from the fire, strain clean, and permit it to cool and clear. Afterwards take the clearest portion, and put some camphor therein, and leave till it is dissolved. Introduce some of this collyrium to the eye and whatever disease afflicts the eye it will cure it."

Another tenant of the herb garden that has escaped is the **White Horehound** (*Marrubium vulgare*), a tall hairy plant with clusters of small white flowers in dense whorls above the upper leaves. Although rather uncommon in the area, it can be found in some waste places. It was widely grown as a remedy for chest complaints and is still much used as a cough cure. The Physicians of Myddfai used it as a *Medicine for Pneumonia*:

"Take the White Horehound and pound well, then add some pure water thereto, letting it stand for three hours, then strain through a fine cloth, add a good deal of honey to the strained liquor and put on a slow fire to warm; take half a draught thereof every three hours, and let your diet be the best wheaten bread and milk; when thirsty, take an apple, and cover it with good old cider, eat the apple, in an hour drink the cider, and let this be your only diet."

Of interest is the fact that a member of the Merthyr Tydfil Naturalists' Society, Dr. T. F. Holley spent three years at Trinity College, Dublin University studying a diterpene substance, marrubiin, $C_{20}H_{28}O_4$, extracted from Horehound. It could be termed a purely academic project, because marrubiin, a naturally occurring aromatic oil, had resisted all previous attempts to elucidate its chemical structure.

Small scale studies were carried out for six months to find a batch of Horehound containing the required substance. Eventually a Liverpool firm, C. W. Field Ltd. carried out a large scale extraction for Dr. Holley, using 204 lbs of Horehound obtained from Morocco. This yielded 500 grams of pure marrubiin, sufficient to carry out structural studies on the marrubiin molecule. The results of these studies were presented to the University in 1954 for the degree of Doctor of Philosophy, and papers were published in the Journal of the Chemical Society and in other learned journals.

148   White Horehound

149   Danewort or dwarf elder

Most people know the **Elder** (*Sambucus nigra*), which probably has more uses than any other native tree in Britain. Every part of the tree has some good use, none more so than the flowers for wine, champagne and tea, and the berries for wine and syrup. But fewer would recognise the closely related **Dwarf Elder** or **Danewort** (*Sambucus ebulus*), the rather uncommon herbaceous perennial with similar flat-topped inflorescences, but growing only to a maximum of about four feet. Some good specimens grow alongside the roadway on the eastern side of Hoover's car park. It acquired the name Danewort because of a legend that it grew spontaneously from the blood of slaughtered Danes. Dwarf Elder, considered to be a native of southern Europe, was prized for its medicinal value and was probably introduced by the Romans. It was reputed to be most effective in the cure of dropsy, but Culpeper seemed to consider it the panacea for a host of ailments, in opening and purging choler, phlegm and water; in helping the gout, piles, and women's diseases; coloureth the hair black, helpeth the inflammations of the eyes, and pains in the ears, the bitings of serpents, or mad dogs, burnings and scaldings, the wind colic, colic and stone, the difficulty of urine, the cure of old sores and fistulous ulcers. Welsh names which show appreciation of its virtues are *ysgawen bendiged* "blessed Elder" and *ysgau Mair* "Mary's Elder".

Trees

The natural vegetation of the greater part of Britain prior to the invasion of the Romans was undoubtedly forest. It is only of recent years that research has established the right of certain trees to be called native. This advance in knowledge was made possible by pollen analysis. Pollen grains of most plants have characteristic features by which they are easily recognised. Their indestructible coats persist indefinitely in peat deposits and form an infallible way of establishing the presence at a given time or place of any pollen-producing plant. The results obtained from the pollen records show that, following the retreating ice, and when the climate became warm enough for trees, pines which can withstand a great deal of cold, began to move in from the south. There was a time when the whole of England and Wales was covered with them. But as the climate continued to improve and become warmer, the deciduous trees—those broadleaved trees which had solved the problem of surviving the winter by shedding their leaves and becoming dormant—proved the more successful group. The pines which are adapted to the cold began to die out in the south of the country, but were ideally suited further north in Scotland, where the Scots Pines formed widespread natural woodlands. Of the conifers only the yew and juniper are native to Wales and England, and when man began to deliberately introduce alien trees to Wales, one of the first was the pine from Scotland.

The deciduous trees known to have arrived early in Britain were the common oaks, birch, alder, ash and hazel, whilst elms, limes and willows were generally distributed, together with rowan hawthorn, blackthorn, wild cherry, crab apple, aspens and holly. Later came beech, hornbeam, white-beam, wild service tree, field maple and the white and grey poplars.

Where virgin woods have been allowed to remain, as at Penmoelallt woodland and Dan-y-Graig, near Cwmtaf, it is usually an indication of poor land, either steeply sloping, badly drained, rocky or otherwise unmanageable soil. Much of the deforestation of the Merthyr Valley and the surrounding areas is traceable to the early iron-smelting industry, when charcoal was the fuel used. Later on timber was required for the coal mining industry.

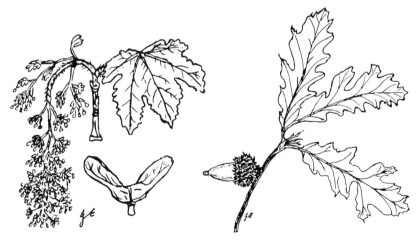

150 Sycamore   151 Turkey Oak

Thus, a very large number of the trees now flourishing in the wild or in parks, large gardens and cultivated areas in our locality are not indigenous but have been introduced from abroad by man's deliberate action. It comes as rather a surprise to discover that such a common tree as the **Sycamore** (*Acer pseudoplatanus*) is probably an introduction of the sixteenth century. Some maintain it may have come in with the Romans. John Parkinson, in his *Theatrum Botanicum* published in 1640 wrote, "It is nowhere found wilde or naturael in our land that I can learn, but onely planted in orchards or walkes for the shadowes sake". Since this time it has spread greatly, and has now become completely naturalized over most parts of the country, not only able to maintain itself but to increase by its very efficient method of winged seed distribution.

Another deciduous tree that is firmly established is the **Turkey Oak** (*Quercus cerris*), many of which grow in the Taf Fechan valley north of Cefn Coed. This is a native of southern Europe which was introduced to Britain in 1735. It was widely planted in the latter part of the century, particularly in the west and south-west of the country, where it is seen at its best. Unfortunately, it has no attraction for the timber merchants or woodworkers, as it shrinks and warps badly, and its only future is as an ornamental tree. The Turkey Oak is readily recognised by the acorn cups, which are thickly covered with "mossy" hairs.

The **Holm Oak** (*Quercus ilex*) a moderate to large sized evergreen tree, is another introduction in the sixteenth century from its native area in the Mediterranean regions. It is easily raised from home-produced acorns and, being extremely hardy, it has continued to spread. There is a fine specimen close to Bethesda chapel in Bethesda Street, which has been the subject of a Tree Preservation Order by the Borough Council.

Another introduction, the **Red oak** (*Quercus maxima*) is a native of eastern North America. The foliage turns to a deep rich red in the autumn, making a lovely sight where it has been planted as an amenity tree in some of the local Forestry Commission plantations. The Borough Council has placed a Tree Preservation Order on a good specimen in the Gwaunfarren Close.

Dotted around the area in isolation is the **Walnut Tree** (*Juglans regia*). It is a native of southern Europe, Greece, and as far eastward as China, but it has been cultivated in Britain from very early times, and it was probably the Romans who first planted it here. Its greatest use is to provide nuts for pickling, when they are harvested before the inner shell hardens. The handsomely marked hard timber is greatly valued for furniture making, and no wood has been found to equal it for gun stocks.

Many people, particularly at Christmas, delight in eating the edible chestnut, either raw or roasted. This, of course, is the fruit of the **Sweet Chestnut** (*Castanea sativa*), borne in a cup which is covered with numerous prickly spines. The tree is a native of southern Europe and was most probably introduced into this country by the Romans who planted it for its

152   Holm Oak near Bethesda Chapel, Merthyr Tydfil

153   A young Red Oak in a local garden
Jack Evans

154   Walnut Tree in a local garden
Jack Evans

155 Sweet Chestnut Tree alongside the road which links Pen-Ddu-Cae Farm with Mount Pleasant   *Jack Evans*

nuts, its shade and its timber which, although inferior to the oak which it closely resembles in colour, grain and texture, is quite durable and a suitable substitute.

A tree in a completely different family, but with a fairly similar English name is the **Horse Chestnut** (*Aesculus hippocastanum*). Possibly everyone nurtured in or near the countryside has played with the seeds in the popular game of "conkers". The tree is actually a native of Albania and northern Greece. The first record in Britain was of a tree growing in 1633 in the famous Lambeth garden of those great pioneers of foreign plant collecting, the Tradescants, father and son.

156 Horse Chestnut

Near the tennis courts in Cyfarthfa Park grows a large tree with an erect trunk and having uniquely shaped leaves, which appear to have had their ends snipped off. This is the **Tulip tree** (*Liriodendron tulipifera*) a native of the eastern half of North America. It first arrived in this country in the sixteenth century and subsequently it has been greatly planted as a specimen and ornamental tree. A very fine and dramatic avenue of these trees can be seen in the well-known and outstanding arboretum at Westonbirt in Gloucestershire.

A tree one would hardly expect to find growing in our locality is the **Fig** (*Ficus carica*) and yet, surprisingly, it flourishes near a foot-bridge close to

157 Leaves of the Tulip Tree, with blossom which opens in June or July   *Jack Evans*

158 Fig tree growing from the footbridge over the river near the caravan site, Quakers Yard
Jack Evans

the caravan site at Quakers' Yard. Fig trees, probably introduced by the Romans, are well established in Yorkshire and in some counties further south. Although presumably imported for its fruit, it cannot produce them in this country, because its special gall wasp *Blastophaga psenes*, which creeps inside the flower to fertilise it, cannot live in this country and no other insect has yet managed to take its place. This remarkable relationship between plant and insect, which works for the benefit of both, is a phenomenon occurring quite often in nature, and is known as symbiosis. This particular tree at Quakers' Yard has possibly arisen from a germinated seed in a discarded imported fig. As some gardeners well know, excellent edible figs can be produced in this country, which form fruit in the absence of gall wasps; but these are seedless varieties, and have no keeping qualities, and are unsuitable for drying.

Amongst the Lime trees, fragrant in flower in the late summer, the only undoubted native in Britain is the **Small-Leaved Lime** (*Tilia cordata*) which in our area is found growing wild on the limestone foundation of Penmoelallt woodland near Cwmtaf, and the Taf Fechan valley near Trefechan.

The other trees we see scattered around the Borough, in parks, churchyards and large gardens, are either the **Large-Leaved Lime** (*Tilia*

159 Common Lime Tree in
Cyfarthfa Park *Jack Evans*

160 Copper Beech Tree in
the Cefn Coed Cemetery *Jack Evans*

platyphylla) or the **Common Lime** (*Tilia x europaea*) which is a hybrid of the Small-Leaved and Large-Leaved Lime.

The Large-Leaved Lime is almost certainly a foreign introduction from many parts of Europe, although some authorities consider it to be native in relict woods on isolated limestone escarpments near Crickhowell and the lower Wye Valley. Although an attractive tree, it grows at a disadvantage in smoky towns, because of the unpleasant blackening of the leaves. This is caused by aphids which feed on the compounds in the leaves and excrete honeydew, a sweet, sticky substance, to which the soot and dust adheres.

Another native tree, the **Beech** (*Fagus sylvatica*) can be seen in an introduced form around many parts of the neighbourhood. The **Copper Beech** (*Fagus purpurea*), where the green colour of the leaves is obscured by a coppery, red or purplish pigment, is reputed to be descended from a single tree that originated as a sport in Germany during the eighteenth century. It grows fairly true from seed, a large proportion retaining the red or purple colouring.

Not a single one of the pine trees or fir trees, with the exception of the Scots Pine in Scotland, are native to this country. Most of them are introductions of the eighteenth and nineteenth century, when large country houses were being built and their grounds and estates were embellished with tall, unusual and beautiful trees. The planting of these conifers became quite a cult, and a whole host of seeds were obtained from North America, China, Japan, Asia, North and South Europe and the Himalayas. This was also the great age of "plantsmanship" with famous landscapers like "Capability" Brown and the many outstanding plant hunters who explored all parts of the world collecting new plants to enrich our flora.

Pine trees and fir trees brought about a marked change in the appearance of the country, which before this time had no large evergreen trees in its landscape. It is only now we are getting the full benefit, by seeing the trees after a hundred or so years of growth in their full majesty and splendour. Fine specimens can be seen all over Wales, particularly in parks and gardens including, amongst others, Bodnant (near Conway), Powis Castle and Leighton Hall (near Welshpool), Stannage Park (Knighton), Penrhyn Castle (near Bangor) and Dyffryn (near Cardiff). Outside Wales, the arboretum at Westonbirt near Tetbury displays a superb collection of conifer specimens.

But to return to our own locality. Growing majestically near the main entrance to the Cyfarthfa Castle museum is a **Wellingtonia** (*Sequoiadendron giganteum*), a native of California, where it has a propensity for attaining great size and age. For instance, the record for this tree is held by one named "General Sherman"; it is 272 feet tall (more than twice the height of the Cefn Coed viaduct), 75 feet around at breast height, and is estimated to be 4,000 years old. So ours is just a baby, possibly a little over 100 years old. The Giant Sequoi, a truly imperial sight, was named Wellingtonia in Britain after the 'Iron Duke' of Wellington who died just after the

THE GIANT SEQUOIA

The sequoia species is an old one. Fossils of them have been found in rocks 140 million years old. Evolving and spreading around the world, these trees became as common as the pines of today and reached their peak of development more than 50 million years ago. During the Ice Age, their range was greatly reduced. Today only three kinds of sequoias survive: The Giant Sequoia of the Sierra Nevada; the Coast Redwood found along the coast of California and Oregon; and the Dawn Redwood of Central China.

	General Sherman Tree Largest Living Thing		General Grant Tree A National Shrine	
Estimated age	2500-3000 yrs.		2000-2500 yrs.	
Estimated Weight of trunk	1,385 tons	(1,256 m.t.)	1,251 tons	(1135 m.t.)
Height above base	274.9 ft.	(83.8 m.)	267.4 ft.	(81.5 m.)
Circumference at ground	102.6 ft.	(31.3 m.)	107.6 ft.	(32.8 m.)
Maximum diameter at base	36.5 ft.	(11.1 m.)	40.3 ft.	(12.3 m.)
Diameter 60 ft. above ground	17.5 ft.	(5.3 m.)	16.3 ft.	(5.0 m.)
Diameter 180 ft. above ground	14.0 ft.	(4.3 m.)	12.9 ft.	(3.9 m.)
Diameter of largest branch	6.8 ft.	(2.1 m.)	4.5 ft.	(1.4 m.)
Height to first large branch	130.0 ft.	(39.6 m.)	129.0 ft.	(39.3 m.)
Volume of trunk	52,500 cu.ft. (1,486.6 cu.m.)		47,450 cu.ft. (1,343.6 cu.m.)	

The General Grant Tree is 30 miles to the north in Kings Canyon National Park.

161   The informative sign, situated near the General Sherman tree   *Mary Thomas*

first seeds reached Europe. The foliage is rather yew-like, where the leaves clasp the twigs which they completely clothe and conceal, and the tree can be easily recognised by its very thick, soft and spongy rust-red bark. It was consequently known locally as the "punching" tree, where you could hit the bark with your clenched fist without occasioning any harm. Other Wellingtonias can be seen in the Cefn Coed cemetery.

A tree of unmistakeable aspect, with its straight trunk, whorled branches and rigid spiked leaves, is the **Chilean Pine** (*Araucaria araucana*) commonly known as the Monkey Puzzle. As its name implies, it is a native of Chile. It was discovered there in 1780 by a Spanish botanist Francisco Dendariarena, while searching for ship-building timber. Archibald Menzies, naturalist on Captain Vancouver's voyage in the Discovery (1792-5) brought back some seeds and young plants of this pine and the tree soon became a fashionable wonder. Good specimens are a familiar sight in many parts of our area, particularly in gardens of the larger houses and in Cyfarthfa Park. Unfortunately, the tree is not very long-lived in this country, thriving best in our moist and wetter localities. The Borough Council has placed a Tree Preservation Order on a specimen opposite the Merthyr General Hospital and to the rear of No. 7 Garth Villas. The acquired name of "Monkey Puzzle" for this tree is intriguing. Apparently, in 1834 a Sir William Molesworth of Pencarron in Cornwall was given a tree for planting, and at a distinguished house party to celebrate the occasion one of the guests, an eminent lawyer, was heard to remark that the tree would certainly present a puzzle for a monkey. Thus the tree achieved its popular name.

162　A photograph taken in 1983 of the General Sherman tree (Sequoiadendron giganteum), the most massive living thing on earth. Standing in the foreground is Douglas Thomas, President of the Merthyr Naturalists' Society　　*Mary Thomas*

163 John Perkins with some of his University Extra Mural group in 1983 attempting to span one of the Giant Wellingtonias in the Sequoia National Park of California   *John Perkins*

164 Chilean Pine (Monkey Puzzle) in the grounds of Pentrebach House
Jack Evans

166   Douglas Fir

165   Ginkgo or Maidenhair Tree

A tree remote from all other trees and plants, closely related to the conifers, and the only survivor of a race of trees that flourished before the evolution of man, is the **Ginkgo** or **Maidenhair Tree** (*Ginkgo biloba*) so called from the resemblance of the leaves to the fronds of the Maidenhair-Fern. One can be seen in Cyfarthfa Park near the tennis courts. Although fossils of this tree were plentiful for a long time, the tree itself was thought to be extinct, as it had never been found in the wild. But it was discovered in the grounds of a Japanese temple by a Dutch botanist in 1690, and the first record of it in this country was in 1754. A hardy tree, it is now grown in many parts of the British Isles.

Another interesting conifer, the **Douglas Fir** (*Pseudotsuya taxifolia*), native to the western regions of North America, can be seen at a few sites, including near the main entrance to Cyfarthfa Park. Trees 400 feet tall and 40 feet in girth are recorded in British Columbia. The Douglas Fir at Powis Castle, by comparison, measures a mere 181 feet by 13 ft. 4 in. (measurement taken in 1960), but probably it is still the tallest tree of any kind in Great Britain.

A small row of decorative trees on the northern side of Cyfarthfa Castle is made up of **Cedars of Lebanon** (*Cedrus libani*), the trees which provided the timber for building Solomon's temple about 3,000 years ago. This tree, as the name implies, originally came from the Lebanon mountains, where apparently it is now rare. It was probably introduced into Britain during the latter part of the 17th century, and eventually became very popular as an ornamental tree in large parks.

Near the main entrance to Cyfarthfa Park is a most striking blue spruce, the **Colorado Blue Spruce** (*Picea pungens glauca*) which, as its name implies, is a native of Colorado. It was introduced into this country in 1862, and has since become a popular garden tree. But because its intense colour is a safeguard against heat and drought in its native habitat, in our damp climate it grows with difficulty.

167 Colorado Blue Spruce near the main entrance to Cyfarthfa Park   *Derek Packer*

168 Cedar of Lebanon on the northern side of Cyfarthfa Castle Comprehensive School
    Derek Packer

The year 1919 heralded a dramatic development in the scenic evolution of Britain. Ever since then the arboreal landscape has been undergoing a remarkable change. During the First World War most of the available sources of home-grown timber had been used in the war effort, and the national need for timber was becoming more and more acute as world demands increased and stocks diminished. Under these circumstances, the State, in the form of the Forestry Commission, which was established in 1919, entered the field and has since embarked on schemes of large-scale afforestation in upland areas. The rate of growth of coniferous crops is substantially greater than that for broadleaved trees, and the financial returns from softwood growing are infinitely more attractive than the slower returns from deciduous plantings. Thus large areas which were swept bare during the War, together with vast open areas in the uplands, were being clothed with conifer plantations. Where once there had been native mixed hardwoods, pure stands of alien conifers appeared and in the more rugged uplands coniferous blocks were grown, sometimes, unfortunately, without reference to the contours of the land or the rivers. In the Merthyr area, particularly around the catchment areas of the reservoirs, where several farms were abandoned, the landscape became thickly afforested. Further south, both valley sides have fairly large Forestry Commission plantations.

Inevitably, when planting trees commercially, the soil, site, altitude and rainfall must be carefully considered in order to secure a reward on the investment. With this in mind, the main species planted in the Merthyr region are Sitka Spruce, Norway Spruce, Japanese Larch, Hybrid Larch and Lodgepole Pine, together with, on a lesser scale, Scots Pine, Noble Fir, Grand Fir and Western Hemlock.

Sitka Spruce (*Picea sitchensis*), native to British Columbia and southern Alaska, is a very hardy tree, thriving even in sub-arctic conditions. It does best where the rainfall is heavy, so it is obviously quite adaptable to our locality. The tree was previously little grown, and little known in this country since it was first introduced by David Douglas in 1831, so Sitka Spruce plantations are essentially a development for which the Forestry Commission are responsible. The tree has been used in afforesting the poorer and high-lying wet and peaty sites, as it is tolerant of poor soil. Consequently, it is now perhaps the dominant tree in this country.

Probably everyone knows the **Norway Spruce** (*Picea Abies*), the young plants being the Christmas trees that decorate our houses on this festive occasion. (Sitka Spruce, incidentally, is relatively unsuitable for this purpose, as the blue-green needles end in very sharp points.) Although the Norway Spruce was native in pre-glacial times it never returned naturally after the ice had retreated. The tree has a wide range in Scandinavia and northern and central Europe and was re-introduced into this country in the sixteenth century, becoming increasingly used as a popular evergreen in estates and large gardens. A well-grown Norway Spruce is quite attractive,

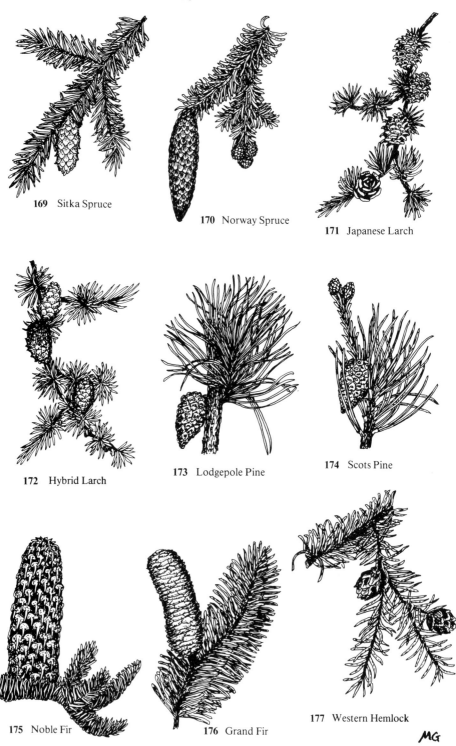

169 Sitka Spruce

170 Norway Spruce

171 Japanese Larch

172 Hybrid Larch

173 Lodgepole Pine

174 Scots Pine

175 Noble Fir

176 Grand Fir

177 Western Hemlock

MG

with its straight trunk and tapering crown of foliage, and is capable of growing to 200 feet in height. It is another tree which grows vigorously in districts of high rainfall, but grows more successfully on the better soils.

The two larches grown in our area, the Japanese Larch and Hybrid Larch, differ from the other conifers in being deciduous. During the winter months they are easily recognised by their rust-red twigs, which look very striking when caught by the sun's rays. Each Spring they put forth that attractive bright emerald green foliage. **Japanese Larch** (*Larix leptolepis*) was introduced to Britain in 1861 from the mountains of Japan, where it grows wild. It is a fast-growing tree, which adapts very well to our variable climate. The **Hybrid Larch** (*Larix eurolepis*) arose by chance cross-pollination of female flowers of Japanese larch by European larches growing nearby. This "first cross" showed a remarkable degree of hybrid vigour, being tolerant of severe weather conditions and growing more quickly than either parent.

The pine that has proved most successful as a timber crop in Wales is the **Lodgepole Pine** (*Pinus contorta*). It is so called because the American Indians chose its straight trunk to support their wigwams or lodges. As a wild tree it grows on the Pacific coast of British Columbia, and up to the timber line of Alaska.

The **Scots Pine** (*Pinus sylvestris*), our only native conifer, is now found in its wild state only in Scotland. Grown singly or in small numbers, it is a very attractive tree, the trunk and branches developing a most striking red-orange shade.

The **Noble Fir** (*Abies procera*) is well-named, as it is quite a handsome tree, with a silvery-blue foliage, and producing very large cones. It is a native of the western coast of America, where it grows to a great size in vast forests. The other fir which can be seen in our local plantations is the **Grand Fir** (*Abies grandis*), which also comes from western North America.

The **Western Hemlock** (*Tsuga heterophylla*) is a very graceful and beautiful tree, introduced into this country from the western seaboard of North America. It is planted only on a small scale in the local plantations, but generally it is very popular as a decorative conifer in parks and large gardens.

Epilogue

We started this natural history section trying to visualize the bleak and barren nature of our neighbourhood at the end of the last Ice Age. This led us to reflections on the initial slow and modest growth of the returning plants, through to some of the changes that were to occur to the plantscape over the next few thousand years. These changes presented an opportunity for a variety of plants from different habitats to prosper, but we have noted that the human influence has played an enormously important and interesting part. The flora everywhere has been altered by the plants that man has moved about, sometimes purposely, sometimes accidentally. One sometimes tends to think that the major effects of man on the rest of nature have been comparatively recent in modern history. Certainly, many of the most striking developments have come since the global movements of the Europeans in the fifteenth century. But as we have seen, man started influencing the plant landscape long before this period. The trees, shrubs and herbs that we now see, either in the wild, or in parks, fields, orchards and gardens, are the species that have either resisted human influence or have thrived with man's co-operation.

The fundamental fact that plants are the only living things capable of making food and thus making man's existence possible, explains the intimate quality of man's relationship with the plant world.

Let our own Dylan Thomas explain it for us, with these memorable lines

"The force that through the green fuse drives the flower
Drives my green age; that blasts the roots of trees
Is my destroyer."

Acknowledgements

The author is greatly indebted to Dr. Mary Gillham who produced the very fine line drawings to illustrate part of the text.

References

1. The Physicians of Myddfai. Translated by John Pughe. D. J. Roderick. Llandovery 1861.
2. British Trees. Miles Hadfield. J. M. Dent 1957.
3. Weeds and Aliens. Edward Salisbury. Collins 1964.
4. Flowering Plants of Wales. R. G. Ellis. National Museum of Wales 1983.
5. Merthyr Tydfil—A valley community (Natural History Section). Dr. Mary E. Gillham. D. Browns & Sons Ltd. 1981.
6. Historic Taff Valley. Vol. 1 and 2. (Natural History Section). Dr. Mary E. Gillham. Merthyr Tydfil and District Naturalists' Society. D. Brown & Sons Ltd. 1979, 1982.
7. Historie of Plants. John Gerard. T. H. Johnson 1636.
8. Culpeper's 'Complete Herbal and English Physician'. Cleave and Son 1826 Edition.